CW00495703

CODE GAMERS DEVELOPMENT: LUA ESSENTIALS

A STEP-BY-STEP BEGINNERS GUIDE TO START DEVELOPING GAMES WITH LUA

A.E. COLONNA

© **Copyright 2023 – All rights reserved.**

The content contained within this book may not be reproduced, duplicated or transmitted without direct written permission from the author or the publisher.

Under no circumstances will any blame or legal responsibility be held against the publisher, or author, for any damages, reparation, or monetary loss due to the information contained within this book, either directly or indirectly.

Legal Notice:

This book is copyright protected. It is only for personal use. You cannot amend, distribute, sell, use, quote, or paraphrase any part, or the content within this book, without the consent of the author or publisher.

Disclaimer Notice:

Please note the information contained within this document is for educational and entertainment purposes only. All effort has been executed to present accurate, up-to-date, reliable, and complete information. No warranties of any kind are declared or implied. Readers acknowledge that the author is not engaged in the rendering of legal, financial, medical, or professional advice. The content within this book has been derived from various sources. Please consult a licensed professional before attempting any techniques outlined in this book.

By reading this document, the reader agrees that under no circumstances is the author responsible for any losses, direct or indirect, that are incurred as a result of the use of the information contained within this document, including, but not limited to, errors, omissions, or inaccuracies.

CONTENTS

INTRODUCTION

Roblox gives builders the tools and freedom to put their imaginations into action.

— DAVID BASZUCKI

The video game industry is ever-growing and constantly evolving. With the development of technology comes an evolution in games. Nowadays, more people have access to personal computers and consoles. As a result, the gaming industry expanded to match that accessibility. Gone are the days when you needed to visit a store to buy a new game. Now, we have online platforms where we have access to a variety of options at the click of a button.

Among these platforms is Roblox. Roblox is one of the biggest gaming hubs, and it's accumulated a staggering 29 million potential experiences. Roblox saw an average of 56 million daily users in 2022, and that number grows by 23% each year. It's no surprise, then, that it has seen more than 40 billion hours of engagement since 2008. With these numbers, you can see why 12 million designers and developers consider Roblox their platform of choice.

Roblox has created a space to build games and publish them with minimal effort. On top of this, it takes the pressure of finding an audience for your product out of your hands by hosting it on a platform that already draws millions of users. Perhaps most importantly, Roblox creates a space to learn and explore. It's free to use and lets inexperienced creators develop their skills and knowledge.

If you're reading this book, you clearly recognize it as the opportunity it is. Maybe you want to learn how to develop games and picked Roblox as a starting point; maybe you want to expand your skill set and diversify your options. Either way, welcome to *Code Gamers Development: Roblox Essentials*. Here, we will discuss Roblox as a platform and explore your career potential with it. We will take a tour of Roblox Studio and use it in practical examples you can follow along with. Together, we'll explore some programming basics and the logical processes of game development with Roblox.

Learning how to make games can be intimidating. With so much information out there on the topic, it can be hard to know where to begin. The programming aspect of game development is perhaps the most daunting of them all, but you don't need formal education or extensive experience to achieve success. All you need is some time, the willingness to learn, and the determination to see it through. With those qualities, you'll be able to learn everything you need to know.

Lastly, know that mistakes are normal. Even the best developers make mistakes. They're part of the process and largely unavoidable. As humans, we don't like making mistakes, but they're not something you need to avoid at all costs. Part of being a successful developer is learning not to fear errors and instead learning to work with them. I'll include some tips on problem-solving as we go and point out some common mistakes and errors you might encounter.

With all that said, let's begin!

1

ROBLOX DEVELOPMENT

Before we can get into practical development, let's take a look at Roblox as a platform, what it means to be a Roblox developer, and what you can expect from it.

WHAT IS ROBLOX?

Roblox is an online platform that hosts a variety of gaming experiences. Despite often being described as such, Roblox worlds aren't games in the way you might expect. It's a collection of virtual worlds where users can collectively share an experience. For that reason, we call them experiences instead of games.

Many experiences are game-like in that they employ game mechanics to fulfill objectives while others are nothing more than a virtual place where people can meet and interact. The truth is that the content on Roblox is so diverse that it's difficult to qualify them as anything other than experiences.

Unlike many other gaming platforms, Roblox doesn't provide individual game files for users to download and install. Instead, it lets you build a 3D world in its virtual environment and then gives users access to that world through its servers and player software.

BEING A ROBLOX DEVELOPER

A Roblox developer is anyone who makes, designs, or contributes to the creation of an experience. Anyone with a browser can become a Roblox developer; it's as simple as heading to roblox.com and clicking on Create. This will give you access to all the tools you need to become a developer (more on this in Chapter 2).

Most people come to Roblox to have fun and experience something interesting. Many users eventually turn to development out of curiosity. Roblox is not only aware of this but encourages it. The founder of Roblox made it with the intention of creating an environment in which users could explore their creativity and interest. As such, it has become a popular learning tool for growing developers.

Being a Roblox developer has many benefits. For starters, it provides you with all the tools and resources you need. Its software is free to download, and you can find a lot of information in its documentation and forums to help you on your way. On top of that, being a Roblox developer lets you practice your coding skills, learn how to solve problems, and express yourself creatively.

Roblox has been shown to promote the skills needed for careers in science, technology, engineering, and mathematics. The things you learn with Roblox can open the door to a future career in making games, web development, software engineering, and even graphic design.

ROBLOX AS A LEARNING TOOL

It's undeniable that our world is largely influenced by technology. As such, computer literacy has become as essential as being able to read. At the same time, coding has become more relevant, too. Many people think of coding as a programmer's skill, something that has no application beyond a career in IT. However, it's an invaluable skill. Without coding, we wouldn't have artificial intelligence, complex websites, or interactable computer systems.

Roblox recognizes this. It combines the creative aspects of building worlds and creating experiences with the technical skills of game design and programming. With Roblox, people as young as seven years old have been able to learn these skills. It's well-known that younger brains are more adept at learning. While they're still developing, our brains are more pliable, making it easier to learn new skills. However, that doesn't mean it's only kids who can learn using Roblox; anyone can benefit from it regardless of their age.

FINANCIAL OPPORTUNITIES AS A ROBLOX DEVELOPER

While Roblox is mostly a tool for learning and creative expression, many developers use Roblox to earn an income. In 2021, Roblox paid more than 500 million USD to developers, proving that there is money to be made here (Landsberg, 2022).

Know, however, that not every developer manages to make a successful living from Roblox. The platform is largely free, and most of its users are children with restricted access to money. This means that consumers are less likely to spend money unless they really want to. The developers who succeed in earning money have been around for years, and their experiences reflect that. Don't go into this expecting an easy income.

Roblox uses a virtual currency called Robux. A person can get Robux by purchasing it through the platform using real-world money or by earning it through sales. If you earn money through your content, your account will receive Robux. There are a couple of ways you can earn with Roblox's monetization setup:

- **Paid access:** A simple way to make money with your experience is to place it behind a paywall. With this, users will make a once-off payment to gain access to your product. Note, however, that this will affect the number of users willing to give your game a try. Most users won't want to pay for something they haven't tried yet. Instead of using it as a tool for financial gain, many developers use this to restrict access to the experience for testing purposes or to create an early access system for loyal users.
- **Game passes:** A game pass is an in-game item that will give users special access or privileges for a fee. With this game pass, the user will be able to enjoy additional content like restricted areas, game buffs, or special items. Instead of restricting access to the experience as a whole,

game passes allow you to limit who can access certain parts of it. Once the game pass has been purchased, those parts become available to the person who bought it.

- **Developer products:** These are items that are available for repeat purchase in your experience. Think in-game coins, energy refills, special equipment, etc. These items are usually related to the experience itself and would give users the option to spend money to enhance it.
- **Private servers:** Roblox hosts experiences on multiple public servers. As users join in, they are added into available servers with other players. You can give players the option to create private servers and control who gets to be in that server. This is helpful when players want to share an experience with friends or for streamers who want to create content without the risk of unknown players. Private servers can be offered at no cost, but many developers charge a monthly fee to reserve a private server as an easy means of monetization.
- **Avatar items:** A big part of being on Roblox is creating an avatar that will represent you in experiences. Many users put a lot of effort into creating the perfect avatar. Roblox does offer free items, but people are more willing to spend

Robux on custom pieces like clothing and character assets. As such, creating catalog items is one of the most lucrative means of monetization. If you submit an item to the catalog and it is approved, the item will be available for users to purchase. You then receive a share of the profits from each sale.

- **Premium payouts:** Roblox offers user memberships. Premium members pay a monthly subscription fee and receive a monthly Robux stipend in return. With premium payouts, you can earn Robux just by having a premium member engage in your experience. The payout you receive will depend on the amount of time members spend in your experience. It happens automatically regardless of any other means of monetization you have but will not occur in experiences that have paid access.
- **Plugins:** Unlike the other items on this list, this one relates to other developers. If you create a plugin that adds functionality to Roblox Studio or its tools, you can publish that plugin on the creator marketplace. There, other developers can buy the plugin for their own use.

Developer Economics

Roblox has a well-thought-out economic structure. In 2022, statistics showed that more than three million developers earned money through Roblox and that they earned roughly 29 cents for each dollar of sales (*Developer Economics | Roblox creator documentation,* n.d.). This statistic is an average and might not accurately reflect everyone's earnings.

To incentivize developer growth, Roblox does not charge any fees to creators who do not monetize their experiences. That means that you won't be responsible for paying any platform fees as long as you aren't earning Robux. Once you monetize your experience, a share of your profit will go to Roblox itself to cover overhead costs and other expenses.

On top of the share that goes to Roblox, there are also other fees associated with monetization, like transaction fees, hosting fees, and marketing costs. In total, you can expect to walk away with roughly 29% of your total profit.

This might seem a little unfair to you. At the end of the day, you lose about 70% of your earnings, but consider this: Roblox is not a site that's meant for making money. It aims to give budding developers the chance to gain experience and hone their skills. They offer free software, the platform to host creations, and the servers and networks that let your products reach consumers. Once developers start earning money from it, Roblox takes a portion of that money to ensure the platform's stability.

The share of profits you receive can vary somewhat depending on how you earn. If, for example, you make sales through the avatar catalog, Roblox would take a larger cut of the profit. This is because the platform divvies up profit between the creator and seller. In the case of catalog sales, you're the creator while Roblox itself is the seller. In the case of in-experience sales, on the other hand, you're both creator and seller and will accordingly receive both cuts.

Converting Robux into Real Money

If you're a member of the Development Exchange (DevEx) program, you'll be able to exchange Robux for real-world currencies. To become a DevEx member, you must satisfy a few requirements. You must

- have earned at least 30,000 Robux. (Roblox differentiates between earned and purchased Robux; purchased Robux will not count toward the 30,000.)
- have a verified email linked to your account.
- be 13 or older.

- be a community member who is in good standing and who has not violated terms of service.
- have a viable DevEx account. (First-time users will be invited to create an account once their application has been approved and they meet all the above criteria.)

If you're not a member of DevEx, you will still be able to earn Robux; you just won't be able to transfer it to another bank account.

TYPES OF ROBLOX DEVELOPERS

While some developers are able to handle entire projects on their own, most are not. As you move beyond the basics, you'll likely find yourself working with other developers on different projects. Each individual brings their own specialties and skills to the table. Based on this, developers fulfill different roles depending on what they do for the project.

The most common types of developers you'll encounter on Roblox include the following:

- **Graphic designer:** This is often the easiest field to get into and the hardest to master. There's a lot that goes into being a graphic designer for a project. It's not just a matter of making sure everything looks pretty. It involves knowledge of color theory, the ability to create an atmosphere with visual elements, logo design, and rendering. Graphic designers are often the ones responsible for creating the right impression since logos and banners are some of the first things users will see when looking at an experience.

- **Scripter:** These developers are responsible for handling the code of the experience and providing functionality to it. This can be intimidating, and as such, many people steer clear of it. While it can be difficult, it's one of the most rewarding roles. Without scripters, we'd be limited in what we can create. It's not as hard as it seems; Roblox uses Lua, a powerful but simple coding language that's easy to learn and master. There are tons of resources for scripters, including support forums and educational material.
- **3D modeler:** Also known as asset creators, 3D modelers create visual meshes to add dimension to your experiences. These meshes can be applied to game items, decorations, or any other visual objects to change the way they look.

- **Builder:** A builder creates the environment of the experience and makes the world in which it takes place. If your experience is set in a forest, the person who creates the forest itself will be the builder.
- **UI designer:** These developers handle the user interface (UI) and create the menus, toolbars, and any other interactable screens. Players use the UI to interact with the experience, and a UI designer is responsible for ensuring that it works properly and effectively while also looking good.

For this book, we'll do a little something of everything. As we move through the practical examples, you'll get a taste for each of these different roles. A well-rounded developer is invaluable. Having the ability to do more than one thing makes you an asset to any team and will let you handle a solo project if you want to. At the same time, being exposed to all the different aspects of development lets you explore your options. As you gain more experience, you'll be able to figure out where your talents lie and find where you fit best. Use this book as an opportunity to try out all these different roles. Feel them out, and you might just surprise yourself with what you discover.

2

ROBLOX STUDIO

WHAT IS ROBLOX STUDIO?

The platform has its own unique development software called Roblox Studio. It comes equipped with all the tools you'll need, including a code editor. It's been described as intuitive and easy to use while still having the power and versatility of any other game engine. Its ease of use is one of its main benefits and the main reason why it's such an effective learning tool.

On top of this, it makes publishing your game super easy. All you need to do is open the File tab, and click Publish to Roblox As. It will then prompt you to fill in the necessary details. Studio makes updating preexisting experiences just as easy. Again, select File and

Publish to Roblox. Instead of filling in new game details, click the Update Existing Games option. This will display all your published experiences. Choose the one you want to update, and it will do the rest.

Another benefit is its expansive community of developers. Roblox is first and foremost a social platform; players meet up with others to share experiences. When you join the community, you join both gamers and developers. With as many developers as the platform has, you'll always find someone willing to share your struggles, give advice, or help where needed.

Beyond the support of a community, you'll also find other resources. If you head over to Roblox's documentation and support sections, you'll find all the information you could ever need.

SETTING UP ROBLOX STUDIO

Before we get started to develop experiences, you need to install the necessary software. In your browser, go to www.roblox.com. If you don't have an account, you'll need to register. When signing up, you'll be asked to provide your date of birth, a username, and account password. If you already have an account, you can sign in. Once this has been done, turn your attention to the menu bar at the top of the screen.

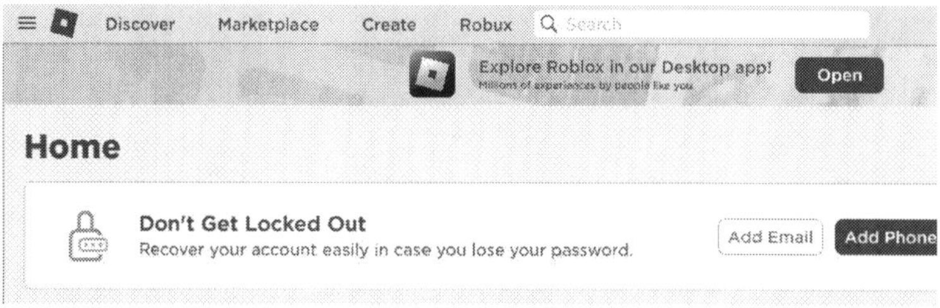

Click on Create, where you'll see a welcome screen with a button that reads "Start Creating" in the middle.

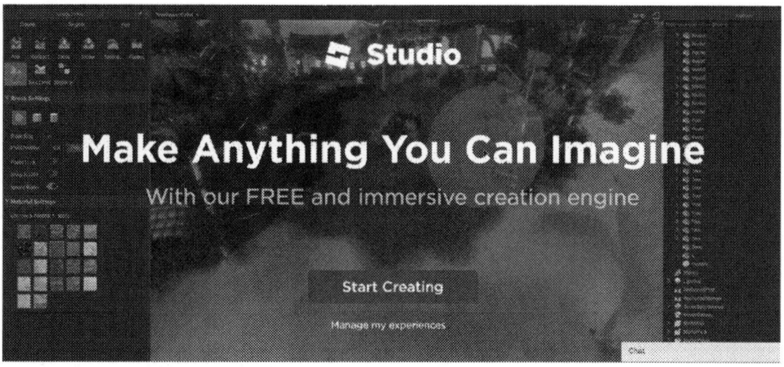

Click on it to launch the program. If you do not already have it installed, you'll see this:

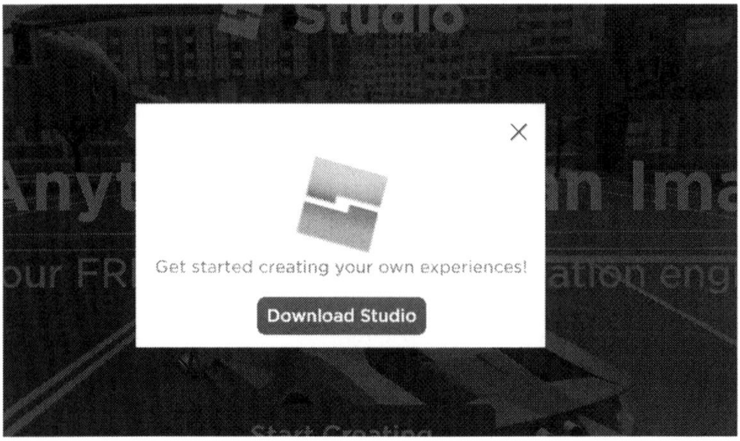

Click "Download Studio" to download the installer. Once it's completed, you can launch it from your file manager.

There are a few system requirements, so make sure your computer meets these before trying to install it. Studio is supported by both Windows and macOS. For Windows, you need to have Windows 7 or higher and Internet Explorer version 11. (If you use Windows 10 or higher, IE will have been replaced by Edge and you don't have to worry about this.) For Mac, you need macOS version 10.11 or higher.

There are also a few hardware requirements. Your computer needs to have at least 1 GB of free RAM, a 1.6 GHz processor, and an internet connection. The last one isn't strictly required, but it helps to ensure that the program stays up to date and lets you back up your progress to your Roblox account.

Once you have Studio installed, go ahead, and launch it.

STUDIO TOUR

When you first open Roblox Studio, you'll see this:

Here you can see the various templates you can use when creating a new experience. The first three are flat, open spaces, while the rest have prebuilt environments. For now, click on Baseplate (the first one) to create a blank project and see the Studio interface.

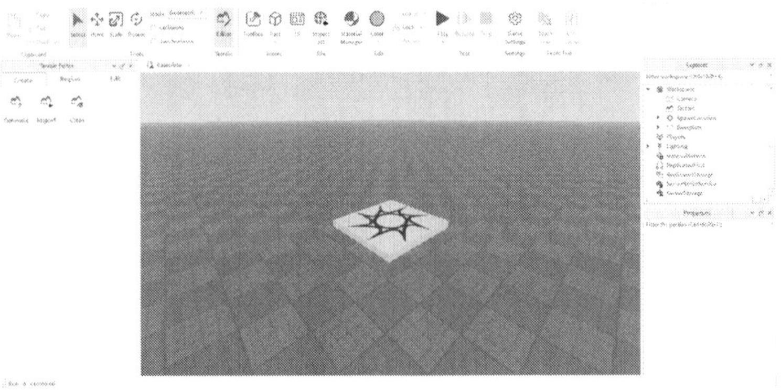

The object in the center is a spawn locator. For now, you can delete it or just ignore it.

This is the basic layout; you can change it at any time by dragging windows around, closing the ones you don't want in your workspace, or opening others.

In the middle of the screen, you'll see the viewport. This shows you what your players will see when they enter the experience. You can look around by holding down right-click and dragging your mouse in any direction. Make sure that your cursor is in the viewport or else this won't work. To move through the environment, use WASD or your directional keys like you would if you were a player.

Tools

At the top of your workspace, you'll find the menu bar. Here you'll find all your tools and various options. We won't cover them all right now, only the important ones.

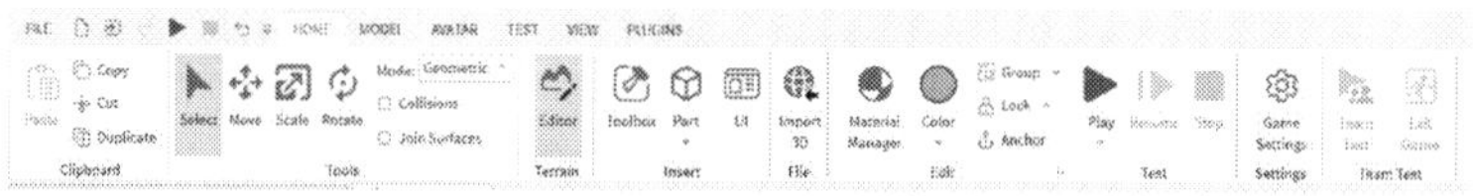

To demonstrate how the tools work, let's add a part into the experience. In the Home tab, select Part, and then Block. This will add a basic brick onto your baseplate.

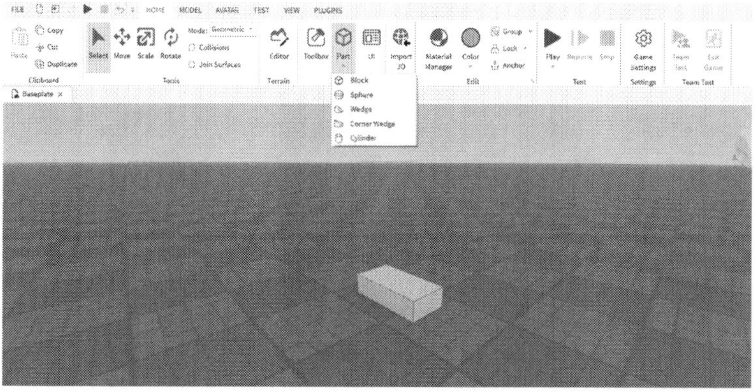

Your first important tool is **Select**. This is the default tool and is used to select parts. When a part is selected (like above), it is highlighted by a blue outline.

The second is **Move**. Like the name suggests, it lets you move a part around. Select the tool from the menu bar, and then click on your block. You'll see this:

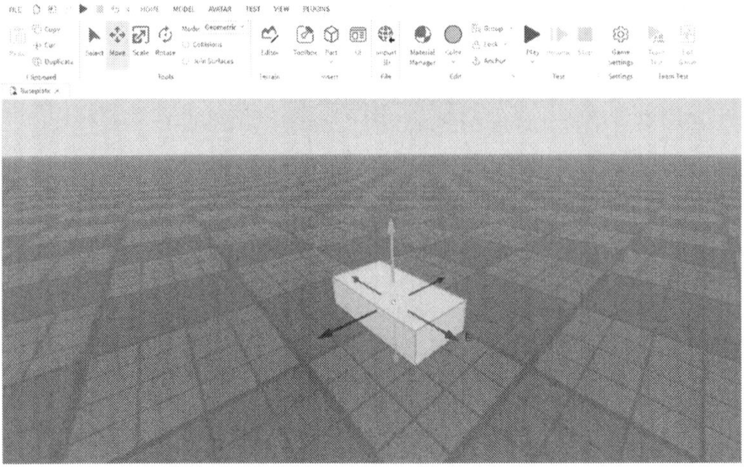

The colored arrows indicate the axes along which you can move an object. Each represents a dimension (x, y, and z). Parts move according to these dimensions. Click and hold the block and then drag your mouse along one of the colored lines to make the part move.

Third, we have **Scale**. Scale refers to an object's size in relation to its environment. Again, select Scale and then click on your block.

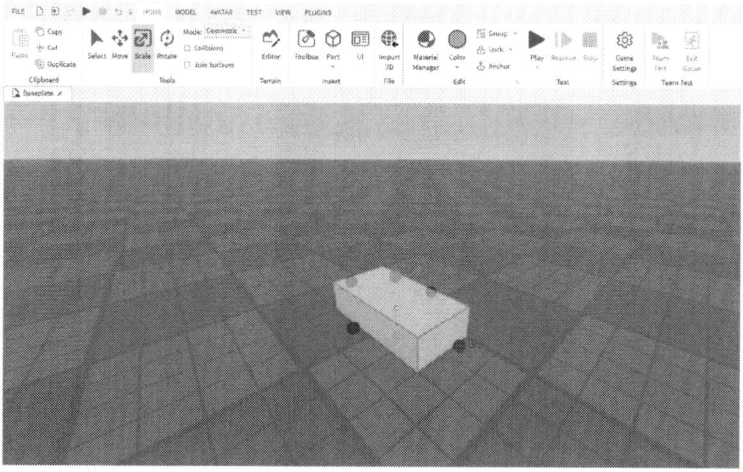

The colored markers indicate the dimensions along which you can scale the part, much like with Move. If you click and hold the green marker and drag your mouse upward, the block will become taller. Likewise, if you click and hold one of the red markers and drag your mouse, the block will lengthen.

Lastly, there is **Rotate**. This tool lets you rotate the part. Like with the others, select Rotate and click on the block to show the visual markers you can use to rotate it.

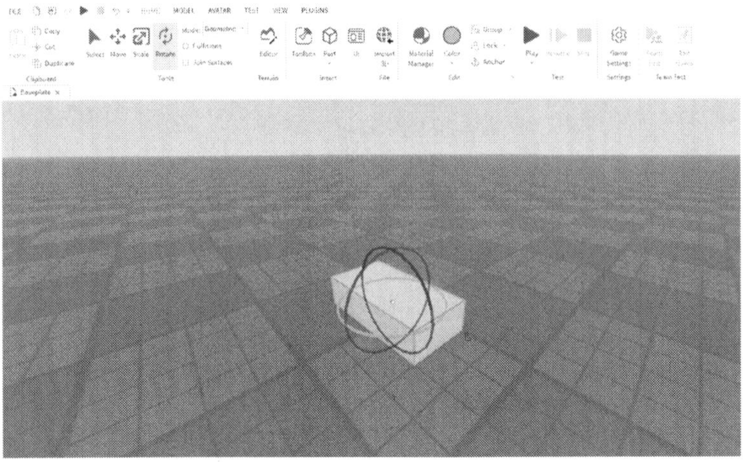

Take some time to play around with these tools. Learn how they work and familiarize yourself with how they affect the block. You can also test them out on other parts since each shape has a slightly different geometry. The best way to learn is to try it out for yourself, so test out the mechanics.

Windows

On the right of the default layout, you'll see your two most important windows aside from the viewport. The first is the **Explorer**. Here you will see everything in a file tree. This window lets you see your project files and structures them into a more convenient setup. As your project grows, this file tree will expand. Instead of combing through your environment to find individual parts, you can instead scroll through the explorer.

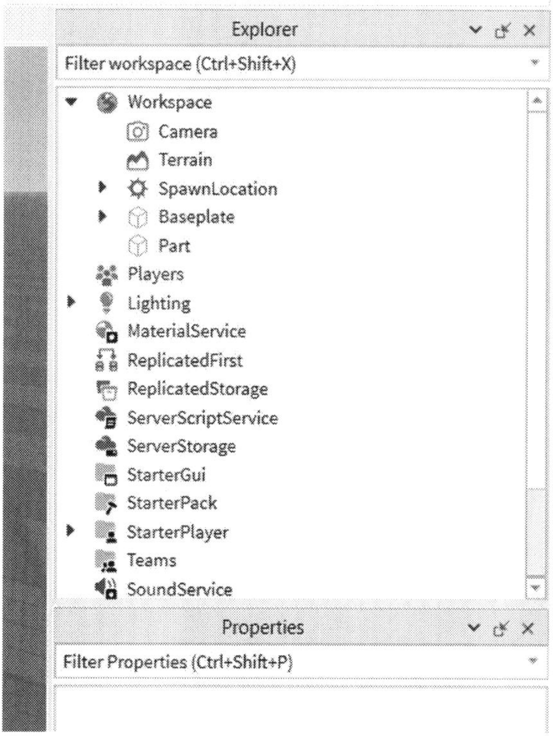

The other one is the **Properties** window. Here you will be able to see the different characteristics of a selected part. If you want to change the color, transparency, weight, or any other detail of an object, you can do it here. If you have a part selected, the window will look like the image below. If not, it remains blank.

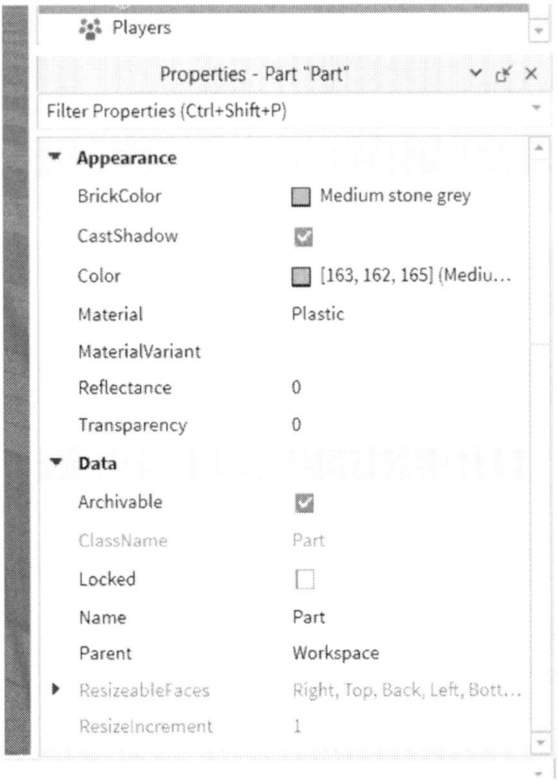

There are also other windows you can open as needed. The **Terrain Editor** is open when you first create a new project, but most developers close it while they're not using it. You can reopen it under the Home tab by selecting Editor.

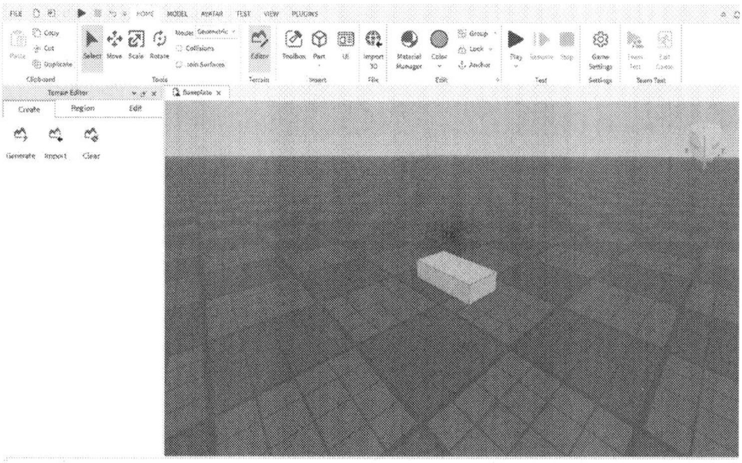

Another optional window you'll encounter a lot is the **Toolbox**. Under Home, click on Toolbox. This will open a catalog of premade assets you can add into your experience.

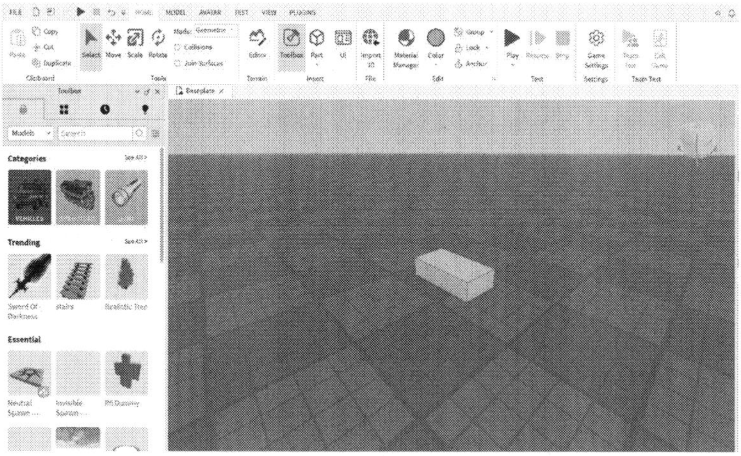

LUA

Roblox uses Lua, a powerful and lightweight programming language, to manage game behavior and mechanics. As a language, it offers simple syntax and easy integration. It was created to extend the functionality of other languages and systems. As such, it's rarely used as a stand-alone language and is instead used in scripting, customizing existing software, and creating or expanding game systems. Unlike many other languages, this one does not create its own forms and applications. Instead, it's embedded into applications created by other systems. In this context, Roblox Studio creates the experience; i.e., the application. We then use code to enhance it and provide functionality that Studio cannot.

Lua needs to be compiled, a process in which code is translated into machine language before it's run by a computer. It uses a C compiler and shares many similarities with other C-based languages. As such, it's highly compatible with most other programming languages and systems. At the same time, it is much simpler and has a significantly smaller learning curve.

What Makes Lua Great?

There are many coding languages, each with its own unique features. So what sets Lua apart from other languages?

1. **Speed:** A language's speed relates to how quickly it can complete tasks, and Lua is considered one of the fastest. It can process complex tasks in short amounts of time, both during testing and at run time.
2. **Size:** Since it's designed to be integrated into other systems, it takes up very little space. In game development, there's a constant battle for storage. Everything that adds to the game takes up space. The more storage it takes up, the more you'll struggle with performance. In total, its source code and documentation only occupy around 1.3 MB of space.
3. **Portability and embeddability:** Since the language is so compact, it can be imported just about anywhere. It's highly compatible with most systems and rarely requires complex adjustments to work with other languages.
4. **Simplicity:** This is an incredibly simple language. It has limited syntax and is easy to read and comprehend, even if you don't have a lot of experience.
5. **License:** Lua comes with a free-use license. It's part of an open-source distribution package,

meaning that users don't have to worry about any licensing fees or infringements.

Pros and Cons

Some of Lua's benefits are that it

- is easy to integrate with preexisting apps and projects.
- is flexible and lightweight.
- has simple syntax, making it an easier language to learn than other more syntax-heavy languages.
- uses a standard C compiler, meaning it can run virtually anywhere.
- uses dynamic variable creation. (We'll discuss variables and what this means in a later chapter.)
- has an active community of developers, meaning there are plenty of documentation, tutorials, and support.

Some of its drawbacks include

- having limited libraries. It might take longer to debug a Lua script than others.
- creating only global variables.

- offering limited pattern-matching support. Pattern matching is a tool used in programming to recognize patterns in data. This is useful for finding errors and filtering large amounts of code. It does not identify patterns but instead finds those it can already identify to increase productivity.

Areas of Use

We mostly use Lua in game development due to its portability and small storage footprint. This is mostly because it is compatible with more powerful languages like C++ (the language used in the Unreal game engine). It can also be added into existing code to optimize the productivity of other languages without risking the integrity of the code that's already there. Furthermore, it reduces the impact of performance on less light-weight languages.

So, other than games, what can you make with Lua? It can be used to develop web applications, developer tools, and extensions. It has even been used as a programming language for industrial programs like *Adobe Lightroom* (an image manipulation app) and *MySQL* (a database manager). Lastly, it can be used by end users to create plugins and extensions for existing software or games. For example, players of *World of*

Warcraft use Lua to create extensions that customize their gameplay.

How Does Lua Compare to Other Languages?

Languages like Python and Java are coding giants. They have so many applications and uses, and they've each amassed a following of dedicated users. While Lua is not strictly a programming language (it's a scripting language), it's still mentioned in the same breath as these giants because it's used alongside them. While it is very different, it still measures up and compares to other languages.

For starters, Lua accepts a variety of coding styles—including object-oriented, data-driven, and procedural programming—while languages like Java are limited to one or two.

Lua and Python share their simplicity of syntax, compatibility with multiple styles, and multi-platform applicability. Python is the slower of the two since it's not a compiled language. Python is an interpreted language, meaning that its code is interpreted on the fly rather than compiled before running.

Lua is similar to Javascript (a web-based language) in that it cannot be used for general-purpose programming. However, it's not limited to web-based platforms and can still be integrated into other products.

3

YOUR FIRST EXPERIENCE – CREATE AN OBBY

An obby, short for obstacle course, describes a game in which players traverse a series of hurdles to progress from level to level. This often takes the form of interconnected platforms and floating objects the user has to jump across. It usually has checkpoints at regular intervals to save player progress and sometimes features a leaderboard to track which players have gone the furthest. They can be pretty comprehensive, with some having thousands of levels.

Obbies are a Roblox classic since they're fairly easy to create and grow. Players enjoy them since they're a great way to pass the time and show off your skills.

In this chapter, we will build a short, classic obby that features a handful of floating parts as obstacles. I will explain each step of the process with images. Follow along and build your own. Use whichever shapes, colors, and layouts you want.

CREATE THE OBBY

Open Roblox Studio and create a new project with the Baseplate template.

Make sure that you have the Explorer and Properties windows open in your workspace. If they aren't, click over to the View tab in your menu bar and select Explorer and Properties to open them up. You can close the Terrain Editor if it is open.

In the examples below, you'll notice that my Explorer is situated to the left of the viewport. Yours will be on the right, above Properties, by default. It can stay there if you so prefer.

Next, turn your attention to the Explorer. In it, you'll see an entry titled Workspace. This represents what you see in the viewport. Click on the little arrow next to it to view everything that's currently in it. In a brand-new project, you'll see four items: camera, terrain, spawn location, and baseplate. Select the Baseplate and delete it.

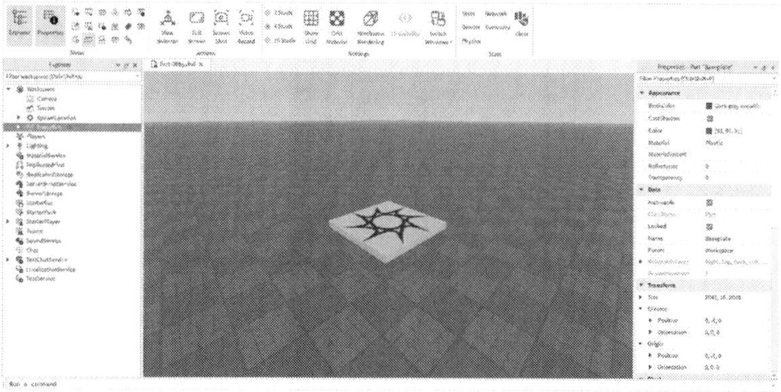

The baseplate acts as a stage on which you can build a world. For this obby, we are going to create a series of floating obstacles and won't need it. Once you have removed the baseplate, you'll see the SpawnLocation floating in empty space.

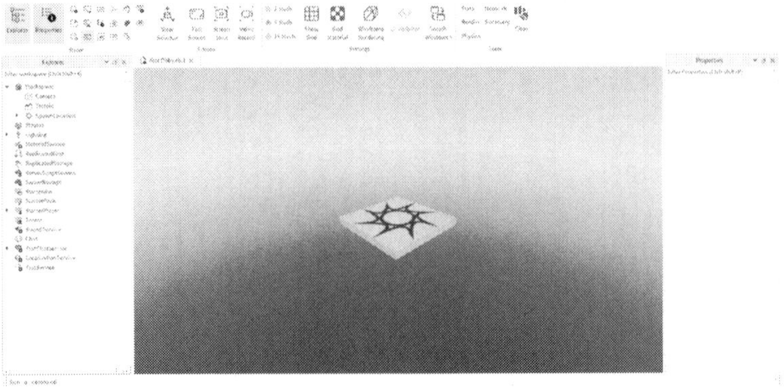

The SpawnLocation object determines where players will end up when they join an experience. It will act as the first platform and starting point for our obby. Once a player has spawned onto it, they can jump from it onto the first object.

CREATING PARTS

Each new obstacle consists of a separate part. These individual parts work together to create the course players will follow. In the Home tab, click on Part and then Block as you did in Chapter 2. The block will appear on or near your SpawnLocation. Once a part is created, you need to anchor it. Select the block and find the Anchor option.

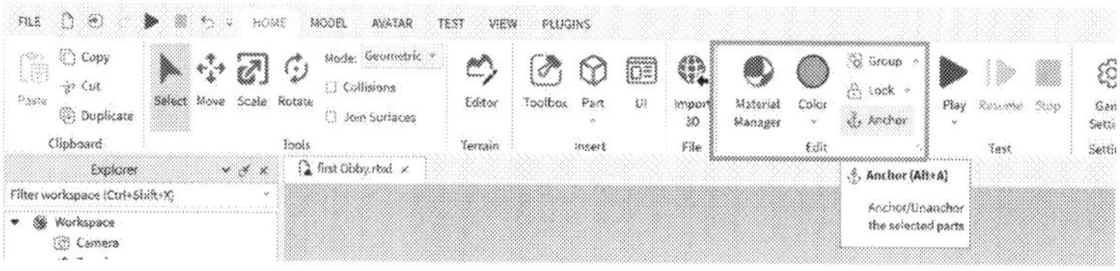

Without a baseplate, parts will fall away as soon as you hit play; anchoring stops this. It essentially keeps them in place so that players can jump across them. Get into the habit of anchoring parts as soon as you've created them. Make it the first thing you do with each new part. Do it before you do anything else. Don't fall into the trap of thinking you'll remember to do it later; you won't.

Now we can manipulate the block with the tools we covered in the previous chapter. Scale it to the size of your choice and move it into position next to the spawn point. It should be close and big enough for a player to jump onto. Mine looks like this:

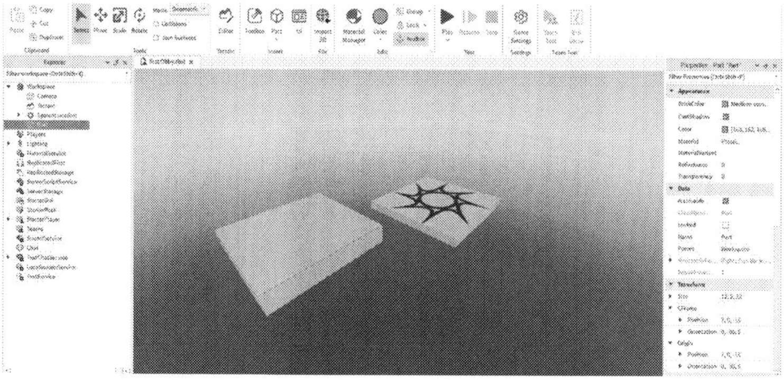

Next, use the Properties window to change how it looks. Select the block to access its properties. Under Appearance, find the BrickColor property.

Changing this will change the base color of the part. Click on the area next to it and choose the color you like. I chose the color Bright blue. Next, scroll down a little to find the Material property. This will let you change the texture of the block.

Parts have a default material of plastic. If you open the drop-down, you'll see a variety of options. Take your time to go through them all and see how they look. I went with Slate, and my block now looks like this:

If you look at the other properties, you'll notice that it has a variety of customizable characteristics. Among them are the Transform values.

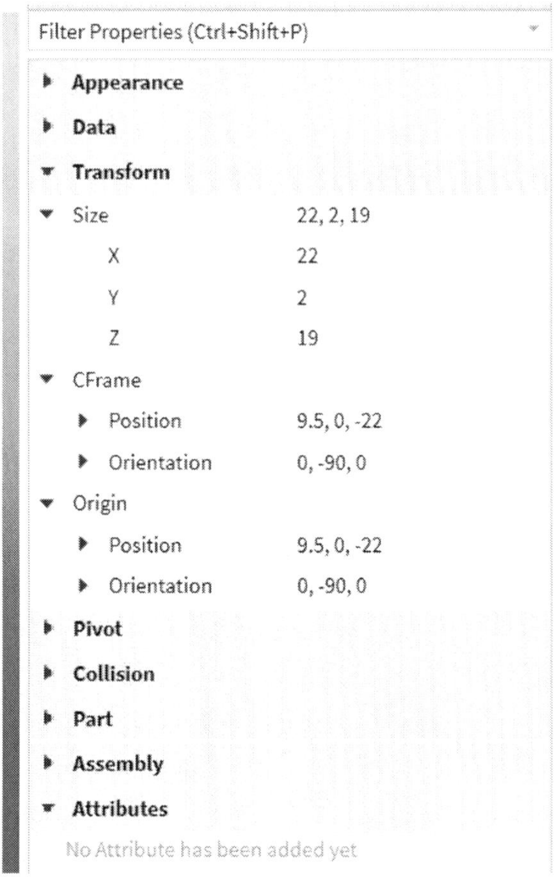

When you used tools to resize and move the block, these values changed accordingly. They represent the part's position and size through numbers. You can move, scale, and rotate the part by entering new numbers into the corresponding values. However, it's tricky to know exactly which numbers to use to get the transformation you want. It's a lot easier to simply use the tools to visually adjust parts through the viewport.

Once you're happy with the first part, repeat the process with a second one. I added a red block with the same material.

This one is a different size and is angled slightly. This is to show you that similar objects can differ from each other depending on how they are transformed and customized. Even though these blocks are the same shape, they look completely different.

Keep adding new parts until you have an obstacle course you like. Remember to anchor your parts as you create them. Use a combination of different shapes, colors, textures, and positions to add variety. How you arrange objects will affect the outcome, and you can use this to your advantage. Add angles and turns to the course to make it more challenging or keep your objects in a straight line to make it easier. You can, of course, lay a series of blocks right next to each other to create a continuous path, but that wouldn't be much of an obstacle course.

As your obby grows, it will get harder to see what you're doing. Use the built-in controls to change how you see the world. Holding right click and dragging your mouse will let you look around without moving. WASD will let you physically move around the environment. You can also use Q and E to move up and down. To zoom in and out, use your mouse's scroll wheel. These mechanics are mostly the same if you're using a trackpad instead of a mouse.

It's helpful to view your experiences from different perspectives. Experiences are 3D worlds; what looks good from one angle might not work from another. Use these controls to move around and inspect your project from all sides.

Once you have enough obstacles, add a final block, and turn it into a flat platform. Change its color to any color of your choice and then select neon as its material. This will create a shining end goal for your players to land on once they have finished the course.

This is what my obby looks like after a few more parts and pieces:

PLAYTESTING

A game isn't fun if it's impossible to beat or too easy. To ensure that an experience is playable, we need to test it. Planning can only take you so far, and it's important to take the time to make sure everything works the way it should. Studio has a play feature that will let you spawn in as a player to test things from the perspective of an end user. To do this, find one of the two play buttons and click it.

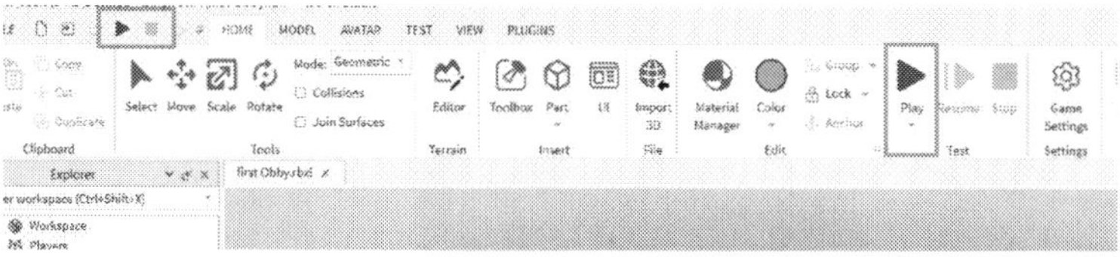

During testing, make sure that your obstacles are within jumping distance of each other, that they're the right size to land on, and that they're all anchored. Any objects that weren't anchored will fall away as soon as the game is run, so this is a great way to double-check that everything is where it should be. Once you're satisfied, you can stop playing by clicking a Stop button, which you'll find near the Play buttons.

PROPER PRACTICE

This is a good place to give you a few tips and pointers for learning good developer habits. The first and most important tip is to save regularly. There are few things as demoralizing as spending hours working on something and then losing all your progress due to some unforeseen circumstances. A lot of things can lead to lost data: the power can go out, your computer can shut down, or another person can interfere. To avoid losing a chunk of progress, get into the habit of saving regularly. When you first create a new project, save it immediately, even if you haven't done anything yet. After that, make sure to save periodically; don't just leave it for when you're done.

Always name your files appropriately. It's easy to tell experiences apart when you only have one or two, but as you grow and learn, you'll start accumulating project files. As they pile up, it will become harder to tell which is which. Good file management is essential, even if you only do this as a hobby. Create a separate folder for your experiences and save each project in a new subfolder within it. Any other file that relates to a specific project can go into the same folder. This way, you keep everything in one place, making it easier to find things like notes, ideas, or plans. Don't just name them "Project1" or "Game2," either. Name them something that describes what the experience relates to. For example, "FirstObby" or "TribeSimulator." Choose a name that will tell you exactly what it is at first glance.

On the topic of naming, name your parts. Each part is a unique object and, as such, should have a unique identifier. Roblox automatically names them "Part." This becomes problematic when you want to use a specific object in code. If they are all called the same thing, you won't be able to reference the correct one in a script. Furthermore, appropriate naming makes it easier to manage your experience through the Explorer. It's very difficult to identify specific objects on sight when they all have the same name or have nonspecific names. Take a look at my Explorer for the obby we have just built.

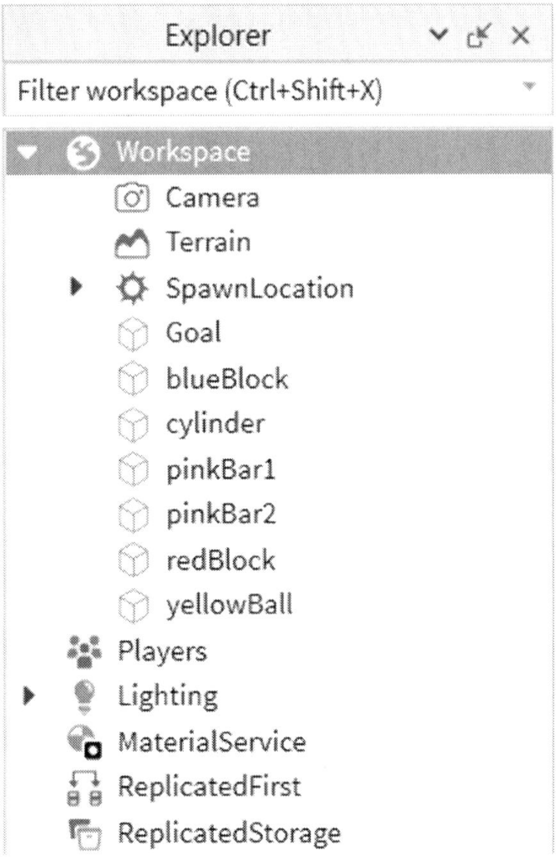

Just by looking at the parts listed, you can immediately tell which object is which. In small projects like this one, file organization isn't as important since we can see the entire experience all at once in the viewport and Explorer. Bigger undertakings, however, aren't as easily managed.

To change an object's name, select the part and scroll down to the Data section in the Properties window.

There you'll find the property called Name.

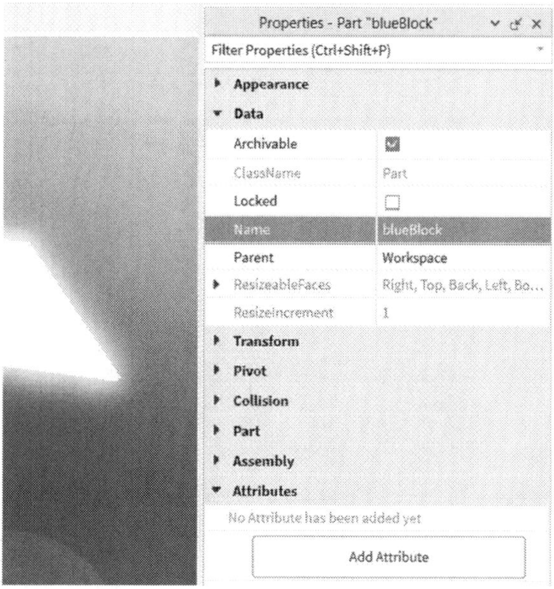

Click in the space next to it and type in an appropriate descriptor. Again, use names that are descriptive.

Of course, no one can force you to use proper practices. Know, however, that we have them for a reason and that they exist to make your life as a developer as easy as possible. Once you start working on more complex projects, these practices will help you optimize your work and productivity. It's a lot easier to form good habits from the start than it is to have to unlearn improper habits and replace them with better ones. Proper practice might not make much of a difference to you right now, but it will begin to matter later in your career—so stick with them for the time being.

UP NEXT

You now have a functional experience. Obbies don't need any fancy functions or features, but you can add a few extra things to make them more fun. To do that, you'll need code. In the next chapter, we'll dive into a few coding basics and explore how to create scripts.

For the time being, save your obby; we'll use it to demonstrate how code works and add onto it as we go.

4

VARIABLES AND OBJECTS

CREATE A SCRIPT

Scripts are files in which we write code to provide instructions for how experiences should behave. They can be used to make provision for things like:

- handling player stats, like health and energy
- item drops
- enemy spawns
- NPC behavior
- environmental changes.

Adding a script to your project is easy. In the Explorer, find the item called ServerScriptService. This is a container for scripts and script-related assets. All objects contained in it will apply to the experience and run if they aren't disabled. In short, this is a convenient place to store general scripts you want to add to your project.

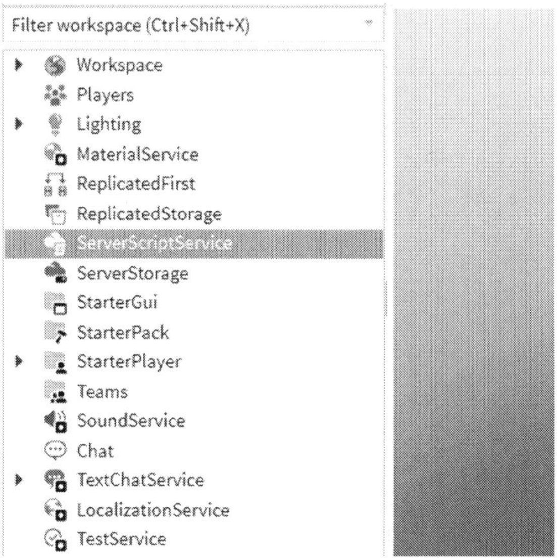

When you hover your cursor over it, a little + will appear next to it. Click on this and, from the drop-down list, find and click Script. You can also use the search bar if you can’t find the right option.

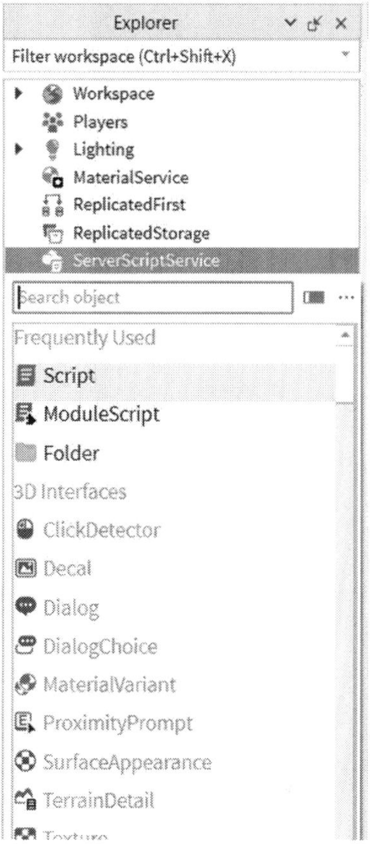

A new script will be added and opened. Rename it "TestingScript." I know it's easier to just leave them as is or name them Script1 and Script2, but that's a recipe for disaster. It's not unusual to have multiple scripts, even in smaller projects. Avoid wasting time having to open and look through all of them to find something by renaming them consistently.

In this new script, you'll see a line of code. It reads: print("Hello world!"). This is a basic line of output code.

Print is a built-in command that tells the computer to display the value contained in brackets to the Output window. This line of code will thus print "Hello world!" into your experience's output when you play it.

To open the Output window, go to the View tab and select Output as below:

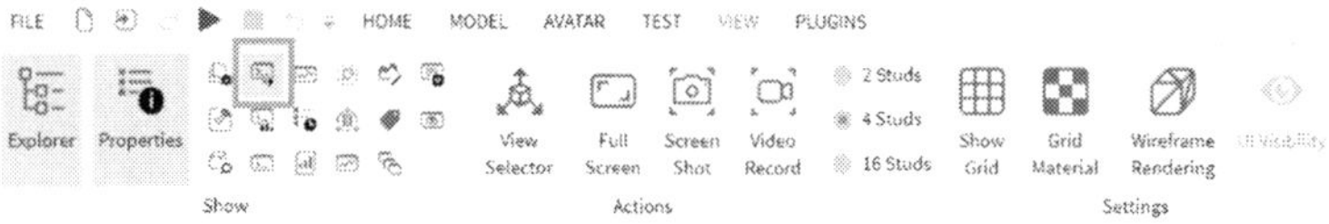

This is a great window to have open in your workspace, especially as you learn how to code. I recommend docking it in the bottom of the screen below the viewport. When you're not using it to check output, you can collapse it using the controls in the top right-hand corner of the window.

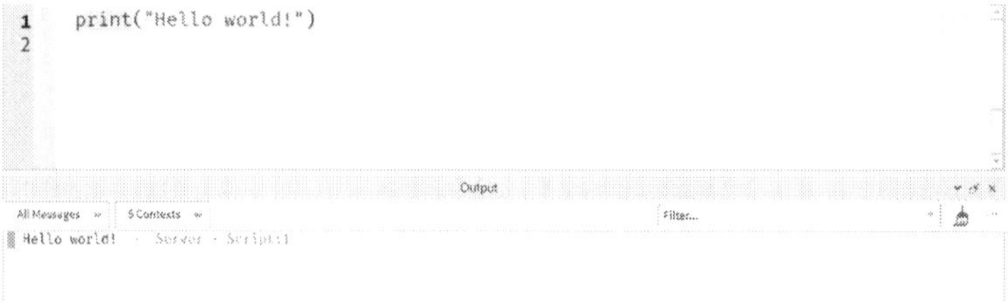

The Output window lets us test code by displaying values and messages. This is incredibly helpful if you aren't sure code is working correctly and need a way to see what it's doing. The displays in it do not affect gameplay at all, so we can use it to see things for ourselves when the experience is run. You'll see in some of the examples below that each output will refer back to the relevant line of code, making it easy to see where errors occur and where to go looking for inconsistencies in values.

CODE STRUCTURE

Before we get into the technical things, let's talk about coding structure.

First, a code compiler does not concern itself with empty lines and white space. You can have multiple blank lines between code and it won't change how it is interpreted. The computer doesn't care about the blank spaces, but it's often easier for people to read code when everything is spaced out rather than crammed together. Add empty lines and blank spaces in your code as needed to make it easier to follow for others and yourself.

Secondly, most characters and symbols used in code have the same meaning in Lua as they do beyond it.

These symbols are called operators, and Lua uses them to dictate code behavior. For example, when it sees "+" it will know to add things together. When it sees "=" it knows that the things on either side of the operator are equal. Most operators can be interpreted the same way in code as they are in normal life.

Lastly, code often contains comments. Comments are lines of code that we do not want the compiler to execute. We use them to make notes and explain lines of code to others. You'll see me use them a lot to explain certain parts of the examples.

To make a comment, use two dashes (--) to preface the statement you want to make. Everything that follows the dashes will be ignored by the computer. This works for single-line comments. If you want your comment to span multiple lines, use two dashes followed by two square brackets to open the comment and then two square brackets to close it (--[[...]]).

In the example above, the lines in green are comments. If I placed a command like print in comments, nothing would be displayed since the computer would ignore it.

DATA TYPES

Values and objects have assigned data types. This is because we do different things with different kinds of information. For example, we use numbers in math, whereas we use words in reading. The same is true for programming. The type of data we work with is determined by what we do with it.

In Lua, there are eight main data types, and they are:

- **String:** a combination of characters put together. Strings are often words or sentences but can also include special characters and numbers. They are always placed in double quotation marks (i.e., "..."). Thus, if you put something in quotes, it will be regarded as having the data type string.
- **Number:** any number character we usually use in mathematics; for example, 1 or 13. Note that it has to be the number and not the fully written-out word. One is not a number, but 1 is. Numbers can include both whole and decimal numbers.

- **Nil:** represents the absence of data and value. It's not the same as zero and is closer to the concept of nothing. The nil data type is applied when there is no value.
- **Boolean:** true or false. It can only ever be one of these two values. We mostly use them to test conditions or check if requirements have been met.
- **Table:** a collection of independent values characterized by an index number or key. We use tables to collect different, unique values that are related to each other.
- **Userdata:** represents a chunk of storage in which UserData is kept.
- **Function:** a unit of code that completes a task. Using functions, we can group lines of code together under one name or identifier. The name then becomes the function, and we can use it to refer to the group as a whole.
- **Thread:** a data type that refers to individual threads of execution.

The last three aren't something you need to break your head over just yet. They do not represent values or data we work with. Instead, they are code objects. For now, it's enough to know that they exist and that they are different from other data types.

The other five, however, are important to know before we get into the next sections. They are the types you'll encounter as values, i.e., the data your game will need to handle. It's important to at least have a basic understanding of the differences between them.

VARIABLES

Variables in programming are placeholders in code for data that you do not have. Think of them as empty boxes that can store information and values. When we want to make provision for data we don't have at the time of coding or data that might change, we use variables to stand in their place.

We do the same thing in mathematics, where we use a variable (often x or y) to represent an undetermined number in an equation until we can calculate what that value is. Programming variables are the same as mathematical variables in that we use them as placeholders for data.

Think about this: You don't know who is going to play your game until they themselves decide to do it. You also don't know what they'll do once they begin playing. Despite that, you still need to make provisions for those things so that your game can handle any players or behaviors it encounters. You cannot explicitly code for every possibility, so we use variables instead.

Declaring and Initializing Variables

To create a variable, we declare it. Declare in this context means to create a name for the variable and use it for the first time. Initialization is when we assign a value to it. Most of the time, these two things happen at the same time, but they can also occur separately.

Each variable has a unique name. This name acts as its identifier in code and is what we use to reference its value. A name can include any combination of letters, numbers, or special characters. Note, however, that a variable name cannot begin with a number and cannot contain any spaces.

Lua reserves the use of certain words. These words have preassigned meanings and cannot be used for other things like names. A few examples of reserved words are:

- and
- if
- or
- then
- else
- for

- function
- repeat
- return

Names and identifiers are case-sensitive. For example, freshWater, FreshWater, and freshwater are three different names. Take note of how you spell and capitalize the names of your variables since you'll have to repeat them exactly when you want to use them again.

For this reason, we use certain case styles when assigning names. There are two main styles you need to be aware of. The first is Pascal Case (hereafter PascalCase). In this style, we capitalize the first letter of each word in a compound name. A compound name is where we use two or more words together; for example, FirstName, BlueBlock, and PascalCase. If the name is only a singular word, it will be capitalized; for example, Block or Calculate. This style is usually used for naming classes, events, and system functions.

The second is Camel Case (hereafter camelCase). The first letter or the first word in a compound name remains lowercase while the first letter of every subsequent word is capitalized. For example, firstName, blueBlock, and camelCase. If there is only one word, it will be entirely lowercase; for example, block or calculate. This style is the one you'll use for most variables and functions.

When you want to assign a value to a variable, use the following formula: name = value. For example:

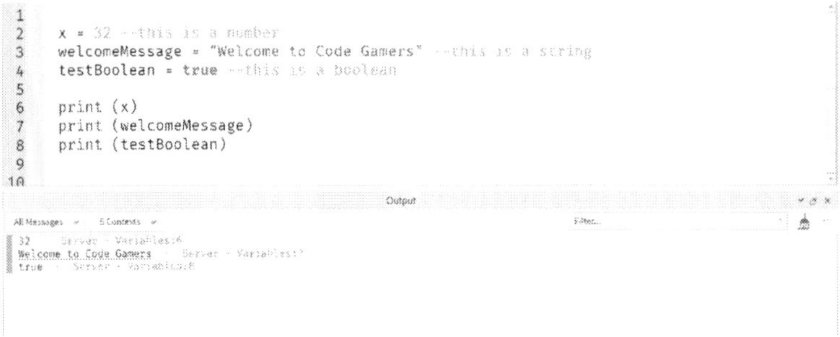

If you want to change a variable's value, you can do so with the same code as you used to initialize it: i.e., name = value. This will override the value that was previously assigned. Using the above example, if I added a line of code to say x = 65 and then printed it, the output would reflect this:

Scope of Variables

The scope of a variable determines where it can be used or altered.

Global variables can be used throughout the entire project, regardless of where they were declared. Unless otherwise specified, a variable will be global by default. With global variables, you don't have to worry about where you can use them or where they were created. If it has been declared, it can be used.

Local variables are accessible only to certain functions and classes. It's almost always better to use local variables since they are quicker to access and more secure. While global variables can be used everywhere, they can also be changed anywhere, meaning there's a higher risk to their integrity.

To declare a local variable, simply preface the declaration with the word "local." Using the example variables from above, I can turn welcomeMessage and testBoolean into local variables while leaving x as the default global.

```
x = 32
local welcomeMessage = "Welcome to Code Gamers"
local testBoolean = true

print (x)
print (welcomeMessage)
print (testBoolean)
```

Variables and Data Types

Lua is known as a dynamically typed language, meaning that you don't have to specify a data type for each variable. The variables themselves do not have an inherent data type but instead assume the data type of their values.

The main data types for variable values are strings, numbers, nils, and booleans. Each value is automatically typed based on how it is described in code. When the value is described with quotation marks, like in welcomeMessage, it's a string. If it has a numerical value, it takes the type number, like x. If the value is either true or false, it is a boolean.

If there is no assigned value, it will automatically take the type nil. If you try to display a variable with no value, you'll get an error.

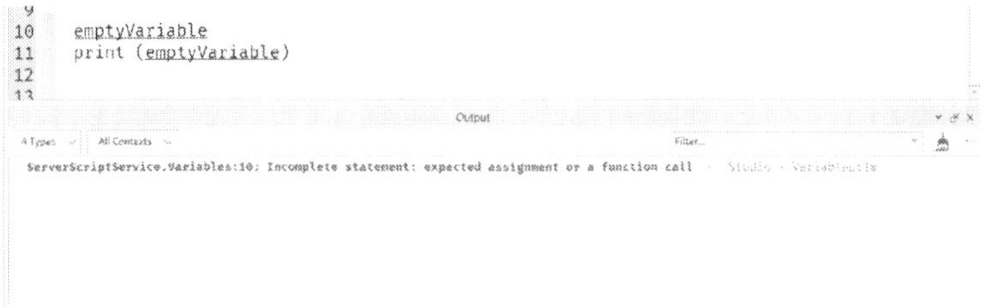

See how the variable declaration is underlined in red? That indicates that there's something wrong. If you look at the output and the red error message in it, you'll see that an assignment or function call was expected. Since the variable was never initialized, it does not have a value, meaning there's nothing to display.

CHANGING PROPERTIES IN CODE

When you first add a part to an experience, it's easiest to modify it using the Studio tools and Properties window. This is because we can see the part and how it fits into the environment. Some parts aren't affected by gameplay and don't need any code. Things like trees and background buildings, for example, can be created and then left as is.

If a part needs to change during the course of gameplay, you'll need to use code to change its properties. This can include visual properties like color and material, transform values like size and position, and others like mass and whether it's anchored. The same properties found in the Properties window can also be accessed and altered in code.

Use the following formula to construct code to change a property:

game.Workspace.Name.Property = PropertyValue.

First, we need the object's location. Before the program can do anything, it needs to know which object the change will apply to. For this, we use the object's location within the Explorer; this is called its path. Parts are contained in the Workspace, and the Workspace is located in the game. Each location is separated by a full stop. Thus, your path begins with "game.Workspace." Add the name of the object you're referencing; hence, "game.Workspace.Name."

Next, identify which property you want to change and add it onto the path. If I wanted to change the Color property, I would add ".Color" to the object's path. If I wanted to change its material, I would add ".Material" instead.

After the operator "=" we need to define the new value of the property. To change the object's color, we use the built-in function Color3.fromRGB( ). This function uses three numerical values between 0 and 255 to describe the red, green, and blue balance of a color. Bright blue (the color I originally chose for this block) has the RGB value (13, 105, 172). You can manually type these values as parameters for the function, but I'd recommend using the built-in color selector that pops up when you type the function.

```
game.Workspace.blueBlock.Color = Color3.fromRGB()
```

Click on either of the colored squares to open the color selector. From here, you can choose one, and its RGB values will automatically be added into the function.

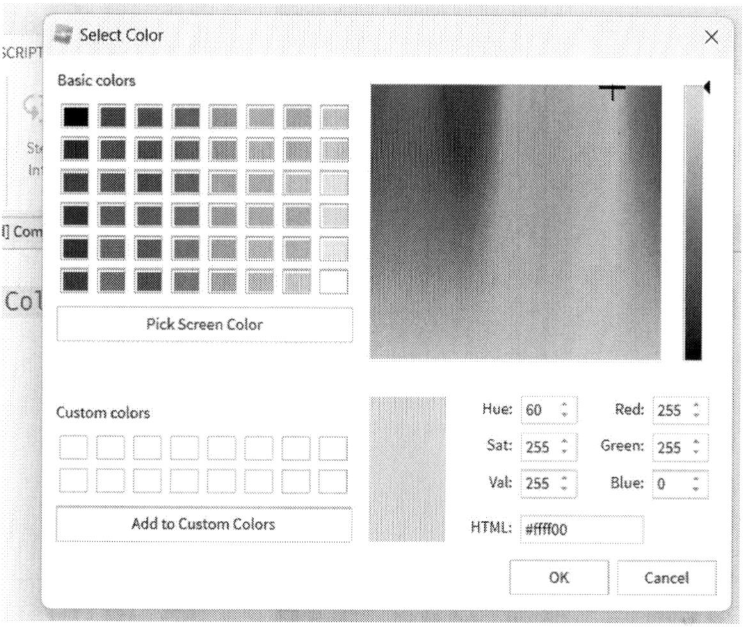

Cool, right?

If I wanted to change blueBlock from my obby into a yellow block, the code would look like this:

```
game.Workspace.blueBlock.Color = Color3.fromRGB(255, 255, 0)
```

Once I hit play with this script enabled, you will see that the block has changed color.

Note that each property has a corresponding value and data type. For this example with Color, the value is the Color3.fromRGB function. For Material, the value would be a string like "Slate" or "Ice." Other properties might have number values, booleans, or other functions. As you type, the code editor will give you possible options as a pop-up. Use them to guide you.

Troubleshooting

There are multiple reasons why your property changing code might not work. The first thing you can check is whether you're using the correct object name. The one used in code has to match the Name property exactly. The same goes for the property identifier. If the property is called Material, you need to type "Material" into your code; "material" or typos would cause an error.

The next thing you can check is the path. Make sure that you have included all relevant locations. You can use the Explorer to check.

Your best bet when it comes to troubleshooting is to run the game and see which error messages you get. This will give you a hint as to what you're looking for. If you don't know how to fix it, copy and paste it into Google and see what you can find out about it online. You can also look for code that's underlined. If you hover your cursor over the underlined errors, a dialogue box will tell you what's wrong.

OBJECT RELATIONSHIPS

Objects in this case refer to everything added into your experience. It can also refer to code objects.

Every part and object in your game exist in relation to others. More often than not, they also exist in a hierarchy. You can see this in the way the Explorer organizes things into folders and subfolders. Take Workspace as an example. It exists as an object within the project itself. Inside it, there are various other objects, like the parts that make up your obby. This is a parent-child relationship. Every object that contains something else is a parent, while everything that is contained in something is a child. In this case, Workspace is the parent, while the objects in it are children of it.

This relationship is mostly organizational, but we use it to our advantage to create reusable code. Take a moment to imagine an obby with thousands of obstacles. Now imagine having to manually code things for every individual part in it. That's a lot of coding, and we don't have the time or patience for that. So instead of providing code for each individual object, we create reusable scripts. But how can we create reusable code for different objects when that code needs unique names? That is where object relationships come in.

Generally, we add scripts under ServerScriptService. While the scripts are attached there, we need each object's unique name to reference it. If we attach a script directly to an object, however, we don't have to specify a unique name. Once attached, the script becomes a child object to the parent part, creating a parent-child relationship between them.

Remember how we can use variables in place of specific information? We can do the same thing here with names. By attaching a script directly to an object, we can use script.Parent instead of an object name or path. If we then create a variable and store "script.Parent" as its value, we can use that variable as a stand-in for the name in code.

To demonstrate, in your obby, click the plus next to any of your obstacles and select script. This will create a child script for that part. I added one to blueBlock and renamed it ColorChange. In that script, create a variable called partName and assign it the value script.-Parent to let it take the part's name. Now this variable can replace the part's path from the property change code.

```
partName = script.Parent
--this creates a variable and assigns its value to be the name of the part
--in this case, partName = blueBlock

partName.Color = Color3.fromRGB(85, 255, 127)
--the variable can be used intead of a path to change the part's color

```

For this example, I changed the block's color to green. Note that it never once mentions the part by name. This is what my obby looks like after I run the game with this script attached to blueBlock.

We can see that the script works, so let's duplicate it. Right-click the script in Explorer, click duplicate, and then drag the copy to any of the other objects to attach it. I added it onto pinkBar2.

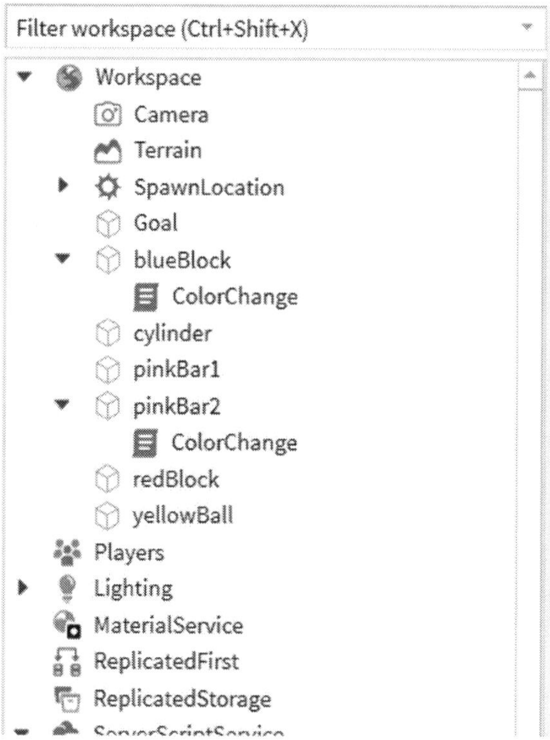

If you open it, you'll see that it's the exact same code. If I run the game, both blueBlock and pinkBar2 are now green.

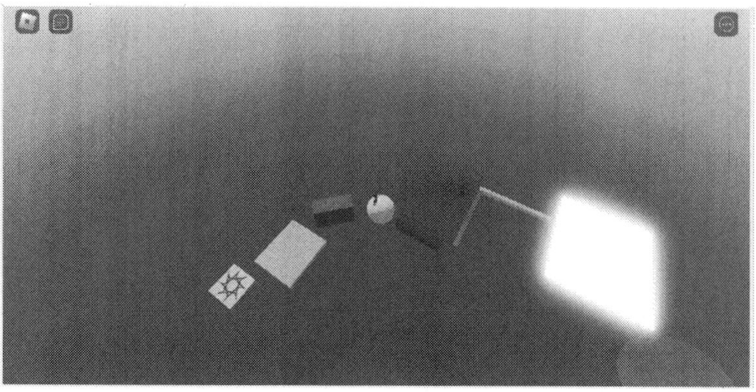

This means that you can use that script regardless of what the object itself is named. This isn't game-changing for an experience like the one we've been building, but it's incredibly valuable in others. With this relationship, we can create duplicable parts and reusable code.

This also only affects the parts to which the scripts are attached. Only those objects change color, meaning that the child scripts aren't affecting the rest of the experience. At the same time, I can still change other objects by using the paths as we did previously.

This method has tons of applications. Let's say you want to create an obby where all the parts change colors together at random. Without object relationships, you would write the property change code for each unique name. Of course, you can still copy and paste it, but you'll have to go through and change the names. With the relationship, you can write it once, duplicate the script, and attach it to each object without needing to change anything about it. This can save a lot of time and effort by giving us the ability to minimize repetitive work.

5

FUNCTIONS AND EVENTS

WHAT ARE FUNCTIONS?

Functions, also sometimes called procedures or subroutines, are units of code grouped together under a single name or identifier. Code can easily become complex and multidimensional. To make it easier to manage, we use functions.

Take a moment to think of an average, everyday task you do often, like brushing your teeth. Think about all the steps involved in it. First, you have to go to the bathroom. Then you have to pick up your toothbrush, open the toothpaste, squeeze some of it out, close it again, and so on. Despite it being a simple task, there are a lot of things that go into doing it. And yet, we can tell someone "I brushed my teeth," and they'll immediately know what it involves.

This is, in essence, what a function is. We can group individual lines of code aimed at performing a single action within a descriptor or name. That name then invokes the various steps and code associated with it whenever it is referenced. On their own, functions cannot execute code. They need to be called for their code to run. To call a function, you use the name you assigned to it.

This makes functions useful for creating reusable code and minimizing repetition. They can be used for a variety of things, like performing calculations, displaying output, and creating objects. Roblox has tons of predefined functions, and you've already used them. Print, for example, is one of them.

There are two main types of functions. One is used to perform actions based on data given to it. These functions are used to do things like display output or change colors. The other is used to take data, process it, and return a value. You can use these to perform calculations, test conditions, manipulate data, etc.

The first step in creating a function is defining it.

Defining Functions

To create a function, you follow these basic steps:

1. Define its scope.
2. State the keyword "function" to indicate its data type.
3. Assign a name (usually in camelCase).
4. Define the function parameters or arguments in brackets.
5. Set up the block of executable code.
6. State the keyword "end" to indicate the end of the function block.

```

local function functionName (parameters)
      --code
      --code
      --code
end
```

Like any other code object, if you want it to have local scope, preface the definition with the word "local" or it will take the default global scope. The keyword "end" is usually automatically filled in once you hit enter after the second bracket, but it's always good to make sure it is there. If your code isn't doing what it should, one of the first things to check is whether or not the "end" is in the right place. Everything between it and the definition is considered part of the function. Everything after it is not.

This particular function will receive data via the parameters and use it to execute code.

Parameters

Also known as arguments, parameters are function-specific variables that store data. These variables are local to the function and cannot be used elsewhere. When a function is called, the parameters store the data provided to the function in these variables.

For example, here is a function that performs some simple math. It takes three numbers (given as parameters), adds them together, and then prints the result.

```

local function doMath (a, b, c)
    local result = a + b + c
    --[[the function takes three numbers, adds them together
    and then displays the result]]
    print(result)
end
```

To use this function, I call it in code. Calling a function involves typing its name and then providing values to each corresponding parameter.

```lua

local function doMath (a, b, c)
    local result = a + b + c
    --[[the function takes three numbers, adds them together
    and then displays the result]]
    print(result)
end


doMath (1, 6, 5) --the function is called and values sent as parameters

```

```
Output
All Messages    5 Contexts    Filter...
12 - Server - functions:6
```

The parameters a, b, and c are used to store the numbers given to the function when it is called; in this example, a = 1, b = 6, and c = 5. The function takes those numbers and adds them together. The sum is assigned to a local variable called "result" and then printed. As you can see, the result is 12. If I changed the numbers I gave the function as arguments, the result would change accordingly.

If you provide more data than expected when you call the function, it will ignore any extra values. On the other hand, if you do not provide enough values, the unassigned parameters will be nil.

Functions do not need to have arguments. If, say, your function gathers data from somewhere else, you can simply leave the brackets empty. Parameters are useful when you want them to process specific information like the numbers above.

You can also use variables as parameters in call statements. For example:

```lua

local function doMath (a, b, c)
    local result = a + b + c
    --[[the function takes three numbers, adds them together
    and then displays the result]]
    print(result)
end

aa = 1
bb = 6
cc = 5
doMath (aa, bb, cc) --the function is called and values sent as parameters

```

```
Output
All Messages   5 Contexts   Filter...
12 - Server - functions:6
```

In this case, the same values are still being sent to the function, they are just contained in a variable. This allows us to use data that we do not have yet or data that changes subject to player behavior. In the above example, if the values of aa, bb, and cc change, the function's result will also change accordingly.

Return

The previous example used a function that only executes code. If we want to use a function that processes information and returns a value, its setup would look slightly different.

```lua

local function functionName (parameters)
	--code
	--code
	--code
	return --value
end
```

A return function takes information, processes it, and returns its result as a value. Unlike the previous example, it will not print the value as part of the function but rather send that result to the code in which it was called.

```lua
local function calculateSum (x, y, z)
	return x + y + z
	--function adds the three numbers when called and returns the sum value
end


print(calculateSum (8, 2, 6))
--the function is called and the result is given and printed
```

```
Output
All Messages   5 Contexts   Filter...
16 - Server - Functions 2:7
```

This is useful for when that returned value is necessary for other code. Let's say you have a function that calculates a player's health after taking damage from an enemy. By using a return function, you can now use the result for other things like further damage calculations, updated player stats, and displaying it in the UI.

Since it returns a value, we can assign a variable to hold that value and then call the function as part of its initialization.

```lua
local function calculateSum (x, y, z)
    return x + y + z
    --function adds the three numbers when called and returns the sum value
end


sumValue = calculateSum (8, 2, 6)
--variable sumValue is declared and assigned the return value

print(sumValue) --sumValue is used to display the function's return
```

```
Output
All Messages | 5 Contexts | Filter...
16 - Server - Functions 2:10
```

Like above, it uses local variables as parameters to store arguments given to it. It can also take values as variables when called.

Methods

In Lua, functions are considered a unique data type. This means that we can use them as members of other objects like classes and tables. When a function is part of another object, it becomes a method. Methods differ from other functions in that they require the object they are contained in to be called as a parameter—much like how we need to reference an object's parent in a path. A method declaration looks the same as any other function, except that it always takes "self" as the first parameter. Essentially: function functionName (self, other parameters).

This is particularly relevant when it comes to Roblox's built-in functions relating to parts and game objects. Whenever a new part is created, it inherits its members from the Instance class. This lets us access all the functions built into this class and is why we can do things like create objects in code, change their properties, or duplicate them. Most of these functions exist as members of each specific part. Therefore, we need to go through the part object to access them.

For example, Destroy() is a predefined method we can use to code the destruction of an object in-game. Each part has an inherent Destroy method, and to access it, we need to path through the part itself. At the same time, we need to supply the part as a parameter for Destroy so that it can know which part to act on. To use it, the code will look like this: partName.Destroy(partName).

This is what sets methods apart from other functions. Methods exist as members of objects and can only be accessed through those objects. At the same time, they take those objects as a parameter.

Lua has a special notation for methods. Normally, we use a dot notation where each object and member are separated by full stops. For example, partName.Destroy(partName).

```
local partName = Instance.new("Part")
--a new part object has been created

--[[code that does somethign with the part]]

partName.Destroy(partName)
--dot notation


```

With methods, we can also use the colon notation to avoid the repetitive use of the object name. For example, partName:Destroy(). The colon essentially tells the computer to infer that the method (i.e., Destroy) should be applied to the object (i.e., partName).

```
local partName = Instance.new("Part")
--a new part object has been created

--[[code that does somethign with the part]]

partName:Destroy()
--[[colon notation,
    automatically fills in Destroy(partName)]]

```

Whenever you see this colon notation in a script or code example, you can thus infer that it is a method that applies to the object named in it.

Methods as Table Members

We haven't covered tables much as of yet, so let's take a quick look at them. Tables are collections of multiple values. Each individual value is a table member and is characterized by a key or index value. The key acts as that entry's identifier. It will look something like this:

```
tableName = {
    --[[members are characterized by an identifying key and corresponding value
        basically key = value
        entries are seperated by commas after each value]]
    member1 = "I am entry #1",
    member2 = "I am entry #2",
    member3 = "I am entry #3"
}
--[[everything inside the { } is part of the table,
wherever the computer sees {} it will know that the object is a table]]

```

Tables let us group related data into one object instead of managing multiple variables. We can also put functions into tables where they become method since they are members of the table object. When you add a function as a table member, its definition takes a different form. Normally, a function definition looks like function functionName (parameters) end. In tables, however, the name becomes the key, and the rest of the definition becomes its value. Since it is a method, it also takes "self" as a parameter. Altogether, the entry will look something like this: methodName = function (self, other parameters) end.

Now, when you want to call the method, you use its parent object and then the name of the method; i.e., tableName.methodname(tableName, parameters) or tableName:methodName(parameters).

```
tableName = {
    --entry1 = value,
    --entry2 = value,
    methodName = function (self, randomNum)
        print(randomNum)
    end,
}
--to call the method
tableName:methodName(5)
```

Callbacks

When we use functions as parameters for other functions, it's known as a callback. Callbacks are no different from other functions. The only distinction is that they are also used as parameters.

Callbacks can become quite complex. They essentially provide called functions with the ability to access other functions (the callbacks) to tell them what to do. This gives the main function access to the callback's code and instructions. It's a little like a game of telephone, so let's break it down step by step. First, a regular function (FunctionA) is called in code. It receives another function (the callback) as one of its parameters. Through that, FunctionA calls the callback. The callback executes its code and returns a value to FunctionA that it then uses to execute its code. By using the callback, FunctionA can thus do what it was called to do.

Callbacks have very few uses in Roblox, but they are one of Lua's most powerful tools. They exist in most other programming languages, but the syntax for them is complex enough that most people don't bother using them. Lua, however, simplifies them enough that they can be used effectively. In general programming, callbacks have a lot of applications, but in Roblox, we mostly just use it to instance new objects. Let's look at callbacks in this context.

Roblox has a built-in object class called BindableFunctions that lets us create functions that can be used across other scripts throughout the server. Unlike regular functions, these exist as objects in the experience and not just as code or data objects. Creating them through the BindableFunctions class also lets us use its members like Invoke. Invoke is a predefined method that lets us dictate what should happen when this bindable function is called.

Let's say you have a function that creates new objects for the game. This function lets you instance a new object with all of its built-in members, assigns a name to it, sets its size, adds it into the Workspace, and anchors it.

First, we create a function called createPart through the BindableFunction class. It needs to be an instance of BindableFunction so that we can access its Invoke member.

```
local createPart = Instance.new("BindableFunction")
--creates a new function

```

Next, create a function definition for it with the OnInvoke method. This will let us provide code for what should happen when a new part is created and this function is called. We can also create the code block for the createPart function.

```
local createPart = Instance.new("BindableFunction")
--creates a new function

createPart.OnInvoke = function(name, size)
    --[[defines the new function that was created and provides
    what it should do when called]]
    local part = Instance.new("Part", Workspace)
    --creates a new object in the game
    part.Name = name
    part.Size = size
    part.Anchored = true
    --assigns properties based on information received through parameters
end
```

When the createPart is called, it instances a new object. It receives two parameters; namely, name and size. These parameters will contain the values that will be added into a new object's properties. In the code, we assign the value in name to its Name property and assign the size value to its Size property. We also anchor the part like we did for all other obstacles in the obby.

Finally, we invoke the createPart function object by typing createPart:Invoke() and passing it the values needed for the new. Altogether, the entire code looks like this:

```
local createPart = Instance.new("BindableFunction")
--Step 1: create a new function

createPart.OnInvoke = function(name, size)
    --[[Step 2: define the new function that was created and provide
    what it should do when called]]
    local part = Instance.new("Part", Workspace)
    --creates a new object in the game
    part.Name = name
    part.Size = size
    part.Anchored = true
    --assigns properties based on information received through parameters
end

--Step 3: call the function to create the part with its properties
createPart:Invoke("Brick", Vector3.new(5,5,5))

--[[example sourced from https://roblox.fandom.com/wiki/Callback
    retrieved in March 2023]]
```

When I run the experience, there's a new brick added into the Workspace.

Invoke is a method and can thus use the colon notation. Without it, the call statement would be: createPart.Invoke(createPart("Brick", Vector3.new(5,5,5)). The createPart function is used as a parameter for Invoke() and becomes a callback for it. Remember that Invoke is a member of createPart due to it being an instance of BindableFunction. As such, Invoke needs to be pathed through createPart.

If you have trouble following this part, you're not alone. Callbacks are hard. Copy this code into a text file somewhere and keep it on hand as a reference for creating new objects through a function. The fact that it includes a callback isn't all that relevant since this is one of the only ways we use them in Roblox.

OTHER FUNCTIONS TECHNIQUES

Anonymous Functions

Functions can be named or unnamed. Unnamed or anonymous functions do not have unique names of their own, and they are usually used as callbacks or event handlers. Like their named counterparts, anonymous functions still require the keywords "function" and "end." The definition of an anonymous function looks the same as a regular function, except without the identifier. In other words, it will look like: function (parameters) [code] end.

The function we defined after createPart.OnInvoke is technically an anonymous function. In that case, there was no need to name it since it was bound to the Invoke method and wouldn't be called on its own.

Functions in ModuleScript

The whole point of using functions is to make code more efficient and organized. Instead of weaving them into general code blocks, we can define them somewhere else. ModuleScripts are special scripts in which we can place different functions. This allows us to keep all our functions in one convenient place and then import them into other scripts. This makes them easier to find if we want to check what's in them or change them. This is also an easy way of making sure that important functions are accessible to other scripts.

You create a ModuleScript the same way you would an ordinary script. Select ServerScriptService, click the +, and find ModuleScript.

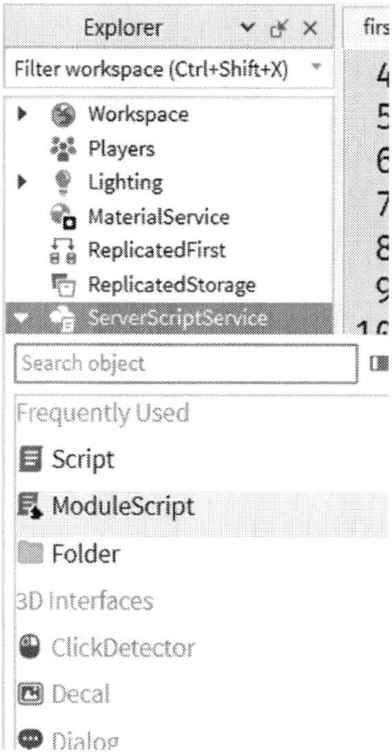

ModuleScripts group functions into a table. As such, they always open with a table declaration. In fact, this declaration will already be in your ModuleScript when you open it. All you have to do is replace "module" with an appropriate name. You can then add your functions into it. To add functions to it, see the *Methods as Table Members* section.

```
local moduleName = {
	--function 1

	--function 2

	--function 3
}

return moduleName
```

ModuleScripts cannot run code on their own. They only define the object in which functions are contained. As such, they need to be imported into other scripts. To do this, create a local variable in your regular script and assign the module to it using "require()." This typically looks like: local moduleVariable = require(ServerScriptService.ModuleScriptName). The parameter for require is the location of the ModuleScript and its name. In this case, it is attached to ServerScriptService. It can also be attached to ReplicatedStorage if it is meant to be used for server-client communication.

If you have a particularly complex experience, you can create multiple modules and then sort functions by purpose. This way, you can group related functions together and keep unrelated functions away from each other. Doing this also means that scripts aren't accessing functions that aren't related to them. For example, if you have a survival game that includes mechanics for farming, fishing, and combat, you can group functions related to each one in separate modules. That way, scripts related to fishing won't access functions related to combat.

Variadic Functions

Normally, functions have a set number of parameters. This doesn't have to be the case. Some functions, like print, can take any number of arguments. Lua also lets you create functions with undetermined or varying numbers of parameters.

To create a variadic function, define it like normal but place an ellipse (...) where you would normally define parameters. In other words: function functionName (...) end. In the code block of the function, you then create a table to index all the values given as arguments when called.

```
local function functionName(...)
--function is declared and ... is used to imply an uncertain number of parameters
    local args = {...}
    --[[here a table is created to store all possible data
    that might be sent as parameters when the function is called]]
end

```

EVENTS

Events are data types that represent the occurrence of something in the experience. Think of things like a player interacting with the game through keystrokes, objects colliding, or anything else that requires a response from your code. Roblox scripting is largely event-based, as is most game development since the whole point of video games is having an experience you can interact with.

Roblox already has a variety of predefined events like PlayerAdded for when new users join the experience or Touched for when objects come into contact with each other. You can also create custom events.

Event Handlers and Connecting Them to Events

When an event occurs (or fires), we use functions known as event handlers to manage them. These functions tell the game what to do when the event fires. The only difference between regular functions and event handlers is that we use the latter for the specific purpose of managing events. We use the predefined method Connect to link a function to an event, thus making it the event handler.

To illustrate this, let's create an event handler for when a new player is added to the experience. This function will get the name of the player and then display it with the message "... joined the game."

```lua
local Players = game:GetService("Players")

local function onPlayerAdded(player)
    --function that displays the name of the player that's been added
    print(player.Name, " joined the game!")
end

Players.PlayerAdded:Connect(onPlayerAdded)
--the function onPlayerAdded is connected to the PlayerAdded event

--[[code sourced from https://create.roblox.com/docs/scripting/events/using-events
    retrieved in March 2023]]
```

Event handlers are largely named to match the event they will manage. We take the name of the event (e.g., PlayerAdded) and add "on" to it (e.g., onPlayerAdded). This name describes its purpose as an event handler for that event. This is standard practice and makes it easier to identify event handlers on sight. For example, if there's an event called RoundStarted, its event handler will be called onRoundStarted.

Disconnecting Functions from Events

You can also disconnect functions from events. In the case of PlayerAdded, the function connected to it is automatically disconnected when the player leaves the game. This is because a new Player object is created for every user that joins. It is through this object that the connection is made. When the user leaves, the object is destroyed, and the function is disconnected.

We can replicate this effect in other events and functions. If you do not want the same event handler managing an event more than once or want to stop it from responding to the event, you can disconnect them using the Disconnect method.

Let's say your code has to manage an event that occurs when two parts touch. When this happens, we want a function to test whether this other part was the target. If it was the target, the function will display "You hit the target!" and then disconnect that function from the event. If it was not the target, the function should stay connected to keep testing Touched events until the target has been hit.

```
local part = workspace.Part
local targetPart = workspace.TargetPart
--objects that represent the parts

local connection
--[[declare a variable that will represent the connection so that we can disconnect
    it within the function itself]]

local function onPartTouched(otherPart)
    if otherPart == targetPart then
    --condition that tests whether collision was with the targetPart
        print("You hit the target!")
        connection:Disconnect()
    end
    --[[after the message has been displayed,
    we can disconnect the function from the event]]
end

connection = part.Touched:Connect(onPartTouched())
--variable is initialized with the value of the connection between event and function

--[[code sourced from https://create.roblox.com/docs/scripting/events/using-events
    retrieved in March 2023]]
```

Note that this script is intended to be attached to an object. It will then test any other part that comes into contact with it.

BindableEvents

Like BindableFunctions, BindableEvents is a built-in Roblox class with predefined members we can use to create custom events. In the above example, part.-Touched is a built-in event. As such, we don't have to provide code to determine when it should be triggered or what it's named. It also comes pre-equipped with methods like Connect and Disconnect.

If we create events from scratch, we have to make provisions for all these things. Creating events as instances of BindableEvents lets us access its members. That means we can use methods like Connect and Disconnect to assign event handlers, and methods like Fire to indicate when the event occurs. Using BindableEvents also gives us the ability to use this event in other scripts.

There are two ways to create a new event with this. The first is to add one the way you would a new script. Find the object you want to bind it to, most likely ServerScriptService or ReplicatedStorage, click the + and then find BindableEvent. You might have to search for it. This creates an event object whose properties you can change.

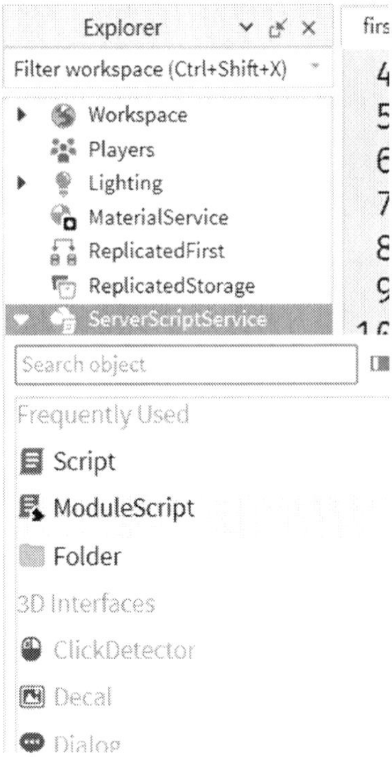

The other way is to instance it through code. We do this the same way we create a new object through Instance or add a new function through BindableFunction. Start by declaring a new event variable and initialize it as an instance of BindableEvents. Once the object has been instanced, set its Name and Parent properties.

```
local newEvent = Instance.new("BindableEvent")
--create the object for the new event
newEvent.Name = "RoundStarted"
--give it a name
newEvent.Parent = "ServerScriptService"
--place it within the ServerScriptService
```

Now that the event is defined, let's write a function to manage it. This function should print a message. Then, connect the function to the event. Since this event is an instance of BindableEvent, we need to add ".Event" to access event-related methods. Finally, define when the event occurs by using ":Fire()."

```
local roundStarted = Instance.new("BindableEvent")
--create the object for the new event
roundStarted.Name = "RoundStarted"
--give it a name
roundStarted.Parent = game:GetService("ServerScriptService")
--place it within the ServerScriptService

local function onRoundStarted ()
    print("Round has started!")
end

roundStarted.Event:Connect(onRoundStarted)
--connect function to the event
roundStarted:Fire()
--fire the event

Output
4 Types  All Contexts  Filter...
Round has started!  -  Server - Bindable event:9
```

Since this is all in one script, I use the local variable in which I created the event to connect and fire it. If you fire it from another script, you can use its assigned name instead. Note that event names are written in PascalCase while variables are written in camelCase.

Remote Events and Functions

Most interactive programs run on a client-server communication system. The server refers to the program itself while the client refers to the user's computer. When a user interacts with the program, the client communicates with the server. The server then processes it through inter-server communication and then responds to the client with output. We usually don't want server-side communication to cross over the boundary to clients, and so we limit the interaction between servers and clients.

Thus far, we've been using ServerScriptService for our scripts, functions, and events. This allows scripts to communicate with each other on the server side of the barrier without crossing over to the client. However, sometimes there is a need for server-client communication. This is especially relevant to events since events are what manage player interactions. For example, when a player presses W, their character needs to move forward. To do this, the client (i.e., the player's computer) needs to communicate the keypress to the server so that the player object can move.

Events that manage interactions like this are called remote events, and Roblox makes provisions for many of them. If you want to create custom remote events and functions, you can do so by attaching scripts and event objects to ReplicatedStorage. If you want to manage them through code, you access the RemoteFunctions and RemoteEvents classes. This comes with its own code techniques.

For more information on this, head over to create.roblox.com/docs and search for remote events.

DEBOUNCE

Some events, like part.Touched, will keep firing. To stop them from doing this, we use debounce to act as a trigger manager. This is a technique that lets us limit the number of times an event can execute code. With it, we can basically put events on a cooldown.

To use debounce in code, we create a boolean variable and initialize it to be false. The first time an event fires, we change debounce to true. While it is true, the event cannot fire again. When enough time has passed, we revert it to false to enable the event to be triggered again.

Let's put it into practice. First, attach a new script to the first object in your obby and create a basic Touched event and onTouched function for it.

```
local part = script.Parent
--create a variable to reference the part to which the script is attached

local function onPartTouched ()
    --function that displays "part was touched"
    print("part was touched")
end

part.Touched:Connect(onPartTouched)
```

If you run it as is, you'll notice in your output that the display message gets repeated for every time your character touches the block. Every step will fire it again. In the time it took my character to move from one end to another, this event fired four times as shown below.

I want to make it so that this event won't fire multiple times but will still be available if I want to return to this block. For this, I use debounce. First, create a local variable called debounce and assign it the value false.

```
local part = script.Parent
--create a variable to reference the part to which the script is attached
local debounce = false
--boolean variable created and set to false.

```

It's important that this variable be local. While it can take other names, it's standard practice to name it "debounce" to make it clear what it does. However, we'll likely have multiple debounce variables per project, and making them local means we can use the name "debounce" for them all.

Next, we create a basic conditional to test the value of debounce. This will check whether debounce is false. If it is false, the code will execute. If it isn't, the test will fail, and the code won't execute. The following code prints the message "part was touched," sets debounce to true, waits for five seconds, and then sets debounce back to false.

```lua
local part = script.Parent
--create a variable to reference the part to which the script is attached
local debounce = false
--boolean variable created and set to false.

local function onPartTouched ()
    --function that displays "part was touched"
    if debounce == false then
    --[[conditional that tests whether debounce is false
        if it is false, the code will execute. if it is true, the event will not fire]]
        debounce = true
        print("part was touched")
        wait(5)
        debounce = false
    end --end of conditional
end --end of function

part.Touched:Connect(onPartTouched)

--[[code adapted from https://www.youtube.com/watch?v=HoZkuvd6RPA
    retrieved in March 2023]]
```

As long as debounce is true, the code won't run. Wait is a built-in function that basically tells the program to wait for how many seconds is indicated in the parameter. In this case, "wait(5)" tells the game to wait for five seconds. Once that time has passed, debounce returns to false, meaning the code can run again.

If you want an event to fire only once, all you need to do is set debounce to true and leave out the rest. That means that debounce will stay true and the condition will fail every time. You can also disconnect the event handler at this point. We'll cover conditionals in more detail in the next chapter.

If you run it now, the message will only pop up once every five seconds if you're moving around. Note that debounce does not mean the part stops being touched. The event technically still triggers. The game just isn't executing the event handler code. This technique helps manage things like weapons' cooldowns, damage mechanics, or spawns.

PRACTICAL EXERCISE – CREATE A BUTTON-ACTIVATED BRIDGE

For this exercise, you want to create a feature in your obby that works as a bridge between two objects. This bridge starts out half invisible and impassable. The idea is to make something players can't walk across until a button has been pressed.

All parts added into an experience have a CanCollide property which means they can collide with other parts. If this is turned off, the player will not be able to stand on it and will instead fall through it.

Add a part somewhere in your obby that will become your bridge object. In the Properties windows, disable the CanCollide property and set its Transparency to 0.5. Transparency lets you enter any value between 0 and 1 where 1 is invisible and 0 is opaque. The higher the value, the more transparent it will be. Make sure it's anchored.

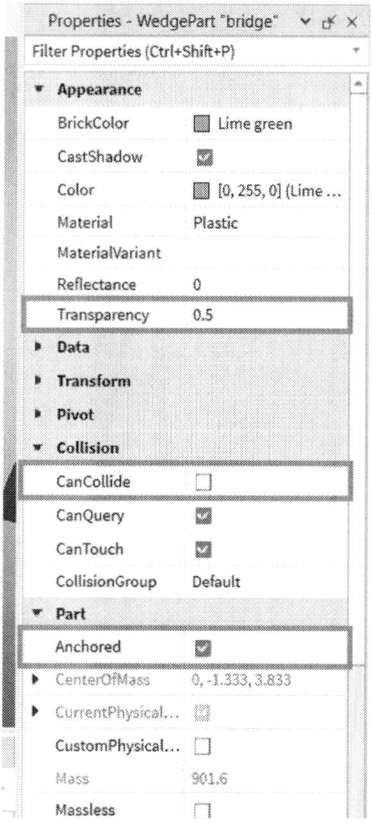

To make this bridge traversable, the player will have to touch a button. Just before the bridge, add a floating brick that will act as a button. Make sure that it is somewhere they can reach and set it to float above everything else. It shouldn't touch any other object. You can also make it red to show that it hasn't been touched yet.

Here's what mine looks like:

Attach a new script to the button object. In this script, create two variables to represent the button and bridge and initialize them. Since the script is attached to the button, you can use script.Parent for it. For the bridge, use its path to identify it (i.e., game.Workspace.bridge).

To make the button work, you will use the part.-Touched event. Go ahead and create a function that will do the following when the button is touched:

1. Change the color of the button to green to show it's been touched.
2. Set the bridge's transparency to 0.
3. Activate the bridge's CanCollide so the player can walk across.

Lastly, add a debounce to optimize the function and make it run only once.

Try this on your own first before looking at the answer below.

```lua
local button = script.Parent
local bridge = game.Workspace.bridge
--variables for the button and bridge
local debounce = false

local function onButtonPress ()
    if debounce == false then
        --function for making the bridge accessible and turning button green
        debounce = true --makes it so fucntion can only run once
        button.Color = Color3.fromRGB(0, 255, 0)
        bridge.Transparency = 0
        bridge.CanCollide = true
        print("button pressed, bridge available")
    end
end

button.Touched:Connect(onButtonPress)
--connecting function to the Touched event

--[[code adapted from
    https://create.roblox.com/docs/education/coding-2/parameters-practice-buttons
    retrieved in March 2023]]
```

Our Generation Has a Unique Opportunity That No Other Generation Has Been Able to Benefit from to the Same Extent – Gaming!

"Failure doesn't mean the game is over, it means try again with experience." Unknown

It's true that there have been some exceptions in the years prior to Gen Z. Steve Jobs and Bill Gates changed the world of computing forever. In the gaming world, no one should forget the contributions made by legends such as Ralph Bear, Jerry Lawson, and Sid Meier.

Thanks to the foundations laid by these heroes, we have the chance to develop code, create games, and even earn money by doing something we love.

The first stages of understanding Roblox were daunting, even terrifying. Despite feeling overwhelmed, you have had a chance to explore this online platform and get confident with the tools it has to offer. You may have even created your first Obby! Kudos to you!

But the learning journey isn't over yet and there are many ways you can still improve your game development and programming skills. Mistakes will be inevitable but the game is far from over. And with some extra help and practice overcoming your coding challenges, the world of opportunities will continue to grow for you.

That's not the only thing that grows! Have you noticed an increase in your confidence? Do you hold your head a little higher after spending time with a community of people that get you?

Think back to a short time ago when you were that student who was constantly told your future depended on your academic performance, just adding to your pressure. Or those days when you keep going to work with no clear vision of your career. Now think of all the hundreds and thousands of young people who feel the same way you did.

All it takes is a few minutes to share your experience developing games to help other young adults achieve the same things that you are.

The great thing about Roblox is that these people aren't going to 'steal' your opportunities. The more people there are learning and enjoying Roblox, the stronger everyone becomes!

Scan the QR code for a quick review.

6

CONDITIONALS

Programs can only be interactive if they have the ability to react to player behavior. Even the simplest games run into scenarios where they need to weigh options to respond appropriately.

WHAT ARE CONDITIONALS?

Conditionals are code statements that let us give programs the ability to make decisions about how to react to certain circumstances. They let us add features like power-ups, rewards, or special events. In other words, conditionals let us tell computers to run certain code if and when specific circumstances are met.

We use conditionals for many things and for many reasons. If something involves some element of cause and effect, odds are there's a conditional attached to it. It's also a very commonly used programming technique —common enough that every language uses them. Like many others, Lua uses an if-statement.

INTRO TO IF-STATEMENTS

A basic if-statement follows very simple logic; namely, if something is true, do this. Its code structure reflects that. It reads: if [condition] then [code] end. Everything contained between "then" and "end" forms the code block and will be executed only if the provided condition is true. If the condition is not met, the code in the block is ignored.

Conditions

The hardest part of handling if-statements is setting up the condition. A condition is any statement where one value is compared to another. For example, debounce == false or number == 10.

Regardless of what the condition is, it always returns the value true or false. In essence, the computer checks the condition and asks itself "Is this true?" A condition succeeds if the comparison is true. For example, 1 + 1 = 2 will be true because one plus one is in fact two. On the other hand, 2 + 2 = 5 will be false because two plus two does not equal five.

We use comparison operators to define conditions. They tell the computer how to compare the values it was given. The most common comparison operators are:

- == (equal to)
- ~= (not equal to)
- < (less than)
- > (greater than)
- <= (less than or equal to)
- >= (greater than or equal to)

For example, if I wanted to check whether a number had a value greater than 10, the condition would be "number > 10." In this case, the condition would be true if the number's value was 11 or more. If I wanted to check if the number's value was equal to 10, I'd use "number == 10."

To illustrate, create a new script and create a variable called score with the value zero (0). Now, code an if-statement to test if this score is less than 10. Add an appropriate display message to check if the code works.

Go ahead and change score's value to something greater than 10 and see what happens.

We can also use multiple variables in one comparison. Say, for instance, you want to compare a player's current and past scores. Create two variables, one for each score value, and create a conditional that will compare them. The goal is to see if their current result is better than the previous one. Provide an appropriate message to display if their current score is higher.

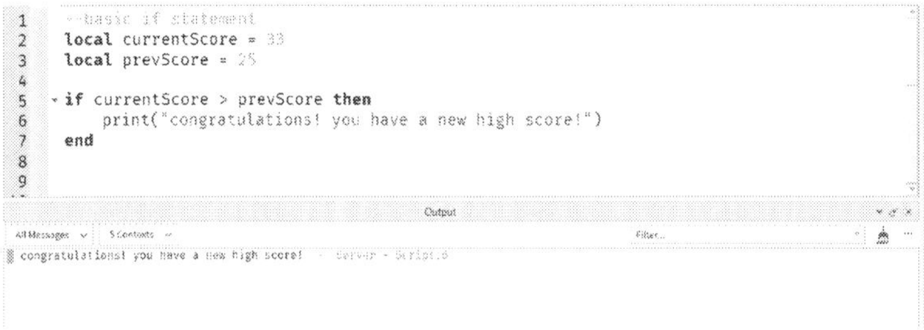

Now let's add something new. If-statements should almost always have a corresponding else statement. Else is a keyword that tells the program what to do if the condition was not met. Simply add else and the code you want to execute before "end" to provide an alternative option.

```
--basic if statement
local currentScore = 33
local prevScore = 25

if currentScore > prevScore then
    print("congratulations! you have a new high score!")
else print("try again")
end

```

Now, if the currentScore is lower than the prevScore, the else statement will execute since the condition failed.

Multiple Conditions

While the most basic if-statement has one condition, you can add two or more. This is for when your program needs to weigh more than one condition at the same time or when it needs to test two different values. By using certain keywords, you can add as many conditions as you want into a single conditional statement.

- **and:** indicates that both conditions must be true for the if-statement to succeed. For example, say a player wants to join a match that has requirements. To qualify, they must be level five or higher and have won at least two previous matches. For that scenario, you can use “if playerLevel >= 5 and victoryCount > 1.”

- **or:** indicates that either one of the conditions must be true. For example, the price of a shop item is 10 gold or 100 silver. In that case, use “if gold = 10 or silver = 100.”

Extra Practice

Practice creating conditions for the following scenarios. Write them on your own and then check the example for the answers. Write code to check if

1. a number is greater than 10.
2. a player’s score is 200 or less.
3. a number has any value other than 10.

```
--answers for practice
local numValue = 0

--#1
if numValue > 10 then
    --
end

--#2
if numValue <= 200 then
    --
end

--#3
if numValue ~= 10 then
    --
end
```

PRACTICAL EXERCISE USING TRAPS

Let's use conditionals to set a trap in your obby. Add a new object to act as the base of your trap and name it accordingly (mine is trapBase). Add another object onto it to act as the trap itself (trapPart). Make sure the parts look different enough that the trap stands out. Play around with colors and textures to make it look dangerous. The point of the trap part will be to kill the player if they touch it.

Move the base and trap parts around so that a player would have to maneuver around the trap to get around it. Make it as hard or as easy as you want.

Attach a script to trapPart. In it, create a variable that will represent the trap. For convenience, I named the variable the same as the part itself. Go ahead and create code for the .Touched event and event handler, and add a line of print code to test if it works. Try doing this yourself. You can look at previous examples if you need to, but really give it a try before looking at the example below.

```
local trapPart = script.Parent
--assign code object for trap

local function onTouch (otherPart)
    print("trap was touched")
end

trapPart.Touched:Connect(onTouch)
```

If you run it as is, the event will fire immediately since the trapPart is touching the base. For an easy fix, go into your Explorer, find the base part, and look at its properties. Under Collision, you'll find a property called CanTouch. As implied, this determines whether or not the part can touch other objects. You can disable this property to make sure it doesn't trigger the Touched event for now, although the code we add in later will also fix this.

Now comes the tricky part. This trap is meant to react to player characters, but how do we distinguish players from other objects?

Let's take a moment to talk about how Roblox handles players. Roblox avatars aren't a single unified object.

Instead, they're collections of individual parts. Each limb, clothing item, accessory, and feature is a unique object—each with its own properties and abilities.

Go back to your obby, run the game, and take a look at the Explorer. In Workspace, there will be a new object added for your character. If you open it, you'll see a whole list of child objects.

When a player comes into contact with other objects, each individual part of the avatar registers as a unique touch. In other words, each body part or clothing item touches the trap separately. This is why we get multiple outputs like this:

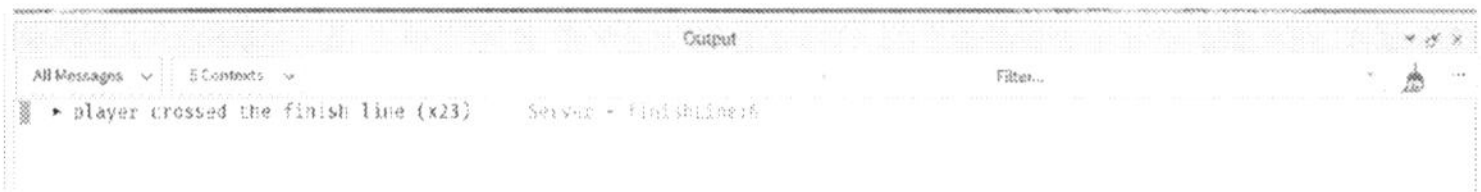

The onTouch function takes otherPart as its parameter. In our case, otherPart takes the value of the object that touched the trap, likely a limb or clothing item. If, say, my character's LeftFoot set off the event, otherPart will be LeftFoot, but that doesn't help us. We still need to test whether or not otherPart is a player character, and we can't do that with a foot or hand.

For that reason, we create a function-local variable called character and assign it the value otherPart.Parent. That means that character will be whatever object otherPart is attached to. In other words, character will reference the player object. This is important because player objects automatically have a child called "Humanoid."

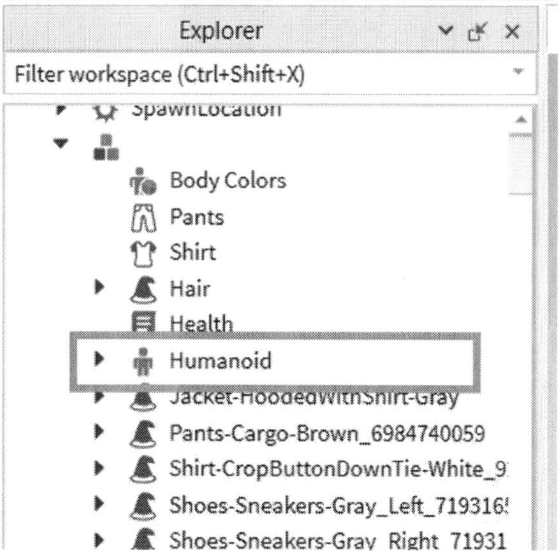

All avatars come with this child and it's highly unlikely that you'll see other objects with this feature. That means that we can use Humanoid to test whether or not the part that touched the trap was a player. To use this in a condition, we first need a way to locate the Humanoid part in our character.

Roblox has a predefined method called FindFirstChild-WhichIsA that lets us search through an object's children to find a specific one. First, create a second local variable called humanoid in the function and add "character:FindFirstChildWhichIsA("Humanoid")" as its value. This will prompt the program to search for a Humanoid child in character. If it finds one, it will store the reference to that object in our humanoid variable. If it cannot find one, the variable will be nil.

```
local function onTouch (otherPart)
    print("trap was touched")
    local character = otherPart.Parent
    local humanoid = character:FindFirstChildWhichIsA("Humanoid")
end

```

Now that we have humanoid, we can create the if-statement to test for a player's touch.

```
local trapPart = script.Parent
--assign code object for trap

local function onTouch (otherPart)
    print("trap was touched")
    local character = otherPart.Parent
    local humanoid = character:FindFirstChildWhichIsA("Humanoid")
    if humanoid then
        --conditional that checks if otherPart is a humanoid character
        print ("trap was touched by a player")
    end
end

trapPart.Touched:Connect(onTouch)

--[[code sourced from
https://create.roblox.com/docs/education/coding-3/traps-with-if-statements
retrieved in March 2023]]
```

The statement "if humanoid then" tests whether or not the variable humanoid contains a value. The condition "if humanoid then" means the same as "if humanoid ~= nil then." Nils will fail this condition since they are the absence of a value. Thus, if there was no Humanoid child in character, it would not pass the if-statement and the trap would not be sprung.

Run the game with this code and test whether or not you can see the display message when you touch the part. If it does not work, check that

- the touched event is connected to the right function.
- there is an end for both the function and if-statement.
- everything is capitalized and spelled correctly.
- all brackets that were opened were closed. If you have two "(" you should have two ")."

Changing Player Health

The same Humanoid object that lets us recognize player objects also lets us manipulate stats like their health. If you select the Humanoid object and look at its properties, you'll see all the characteristics of a player in a game. Things like health, walking speed, and movement properties can all be found here. It is thus through the Humanoid that we can make objects kill players or otherwise affect their abilities.

Player characters die when their health reaches zero. This is built into Studio. All we have to do is write code to set the player's health to zero when they touch the trap.

In your if-statement, add the following code: humanoid.Health = 0. Hit play and see what happens.

```
local function onTouch (otherPart)
    print("trap was touched")
    local character = otherPart.Parent
    local humanoid = character:FindFirstChildWhichIsA("Humanoid")
    if humanoid then
        --conditional that checks if otherPart is a humanoid character
        print ("trap was touched by a player")
        humanoid.Health = 0
        --kills the character
    end
end
```

Once the Touched event is fired, onTouch will check whether the object that triggered it contains a Humanoid object. If it does, that part's Health property will be set to zero, which kills the player. If it does not, nothing will happen.

EXTRA PRACTICE

Use what you learned in the previous example and try to create a power-up feature. Add the following features:

- Once a certain object is touched, the player's speed increases temporarily.
- The power-up disappears once it's been touched.
- The power-up effect should go away after a few seconds.

MULTIPLE CONDITIONS WITH ELSEIF

An elseif is basically a collection of if-statements grouped together with which you can set out various alternative conditions that can be tested if the first one does not succeed.

```
--example elseif that tests a value against multiple options
numValue = 3

if numValue == 1 then --first condition
    print("first")
elseif numValue == 2 then --second option
    print("second")
elseif numValue == 3 then --third option
    print("third")
elseif numValue == 4 then --fourth condition
    print("fourth")
elseif numValue == 5 then --fifth condition
    print("fifth")
else --if none of the conditions were true, do this
    print("sorry, wrong number")
end
```

For example, the above code will first test if a number is equal to one. If it's not, it will move on through the list until it gets to the end or finds a match for numValue.

PRACTICAL EXERCISE WITH ELSEIF

To illustrate an elseif properly, let's add a race to the obby. You can create a whole new project if you want or add an additional section into your obby. Alternatively, you can just use the one you already have. I added a short racetrack onto my obby.

Tip: You can group different parts together into a folder by selecting them, right-clicking, and then choosing Group As A Folder. This makes managing and organizing big projects a lot easier.

At minimum, you need a racetrack and a finish line for the player to cross. I use a block with the texture ForceField for my part finishLine; I also disabled its CanCollide so players can run through it. If you aren't building something new, just use the last part in your obstacle course as the finish line.

In short, this racetrack is going to record how long it takes players to reach the finish line and then give them a reward based on that time. Try this on your own first before looking at the example for the answer. The only part of this exercise that involves new elements is the section on measuring time.

If you have no idea how to do this, that's fine. Here's a hint: For the game to time players, it needs a way of knowing when the race ends. The race ends when players cross the finish line. How will the game know when the player crosses the finish line?

Setting Up the Race

Before we begin, let's walk through the logic of what we'll attempt. While the race is active, the game will time the player. The race ends once they cross the finish line. Mine is an object players have to pass through. Alternatively, it might be an object they run across. Either way, the player will eventually touch the object that represents the finish line. That means that we can use a Touched event to judge when the race is over. However, since finishLine is part of a bigger environment, we need to test whether the event was triggered by a player object before ending the race.

Once the race has finished, we need to see how long it took them and then assign a reward based on the amount of time it took to finish the race. To do that, we'll need to find a way to track time while the race is active.

Since this is all dependent on the finishLine, attach a script to whatever object acts as yours. Begin by creating two variables, one to represent the part and one to track time. For now, assign the value zero to the latter.

```
local finishLine = script.Parent
local timePassed = 0

```

Code the necessary statements to handle a Touched event. The onTouch event handler will decide when the race will end. Only the touch of a player object should end the race. Use the previous example to construct code that will test if the object that touched the finish-Line is a player. Add a suitable display message and test it to see if it works.

```
local function onTouchFinish (otherPart)
    local character = otherPart.Parent
    local humanoid = character:FindFirstChildWhichIsA("Humanoid")
    if humanoid then
        print("player crossed the finish line")
    end
end

```

Create a second function called finish. We're adding a second function to split the workload; the onTouch will determine when the race ends, whereas the finish function will determine what happens once the race is over. For now, cut and paste the print code into the finish function. In its place in onTouchFinish, call finish.

```
local function finish ()
    print("player crossed the finish line")
end

local function onTouchFinish (otherPart)
    local character = otherPart.Parent
    local humanoid = character:FindFirstChildWhichIsA("Humanoid")
    if humanoid then
        finish()
    end
end
```

As it is now, once the part is touched, the event will trigger and call the onTouchFinish function. Here, the game will test whether a player has touched the finish line. If it is a player object, the finish function will be called. It, in turn, will print the display message.

If you run the code now, it will successfully recognize a player's touch, but the code will run multiple times as shown in the output.

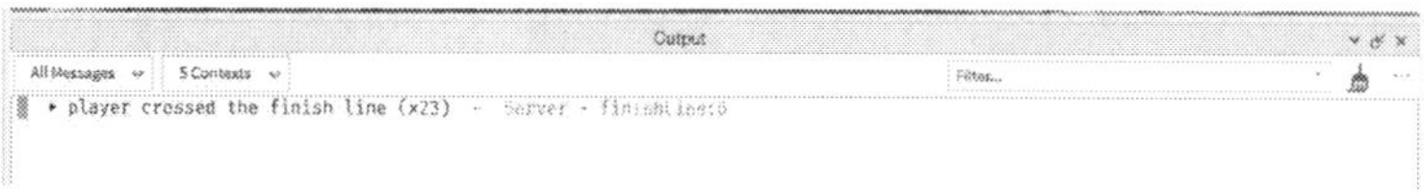

To fix this, we need to add something extra to the conditional. Try to come up with a solution on your own.

Stopping Repetition

If your answer was debounce, congratulations! You're mostly correct. The solution is to create and use a boolean variable that will deactivate the race after the finish line was touched the first time. This uses the same logic as debounce.

First, create a local variable called raceActive and assign it the value true. Make sure that it isn't declared inside either of the functions. As implied, while the race is active, raceActive is true. Once the race has stopped, raceActive will become false. Add it to the conditional statement. This will make the game check if the race is still active before running finish. Next, add code to the finish function to turn raceActive false.

```
local function finish ()
    print("player crossed the finish line")
    raceActive = false
end

local function onTouchFinish (otherPart)
    local character = otherPart.Parent
    local humanoid = character:FindFirstChildWhichIsA("Humanoid")
    if humanoid and raceActive == true then
        finish()
    end
end
```

Now, once the player crosses the finish line, the code will call onTouchFinish. It will check conditions and then call finish, who will then end the race.

Hit play and check to see that the game no longer spams the display message.

Measuring Time

To track the amount of time that's passed, we use a loop. We'll look at loops in the next chapter, so if you have a hard time following this next section, that's okay. The logic in it is pretty simple and works by waiting one second and then increasing a counter. Add the code in the example below to the bottom of your script. This code increases the value of timePassed by one (1) for each second that passes while the race is active. It will keep doing this until raceActive becomes false.

```
finishLine.Touched:Connect(onTouchFinish)

while raceActive == true do
    wait (1)
    --wait 1 second
    timePassed = timePassed + 1
    --increase timePassed by 1
    print(timePassed)
    --display the value of timePassed to test
end
```

The compiler reads and executes code the same way we do, from top to bottom. Our two functions are only executed when the Touched event fires. Touched only fires once the finishLine part has been touched. Until then, raceActive remains true. Neither function will be called until onTouch has been connected to the event. If the loop is above the Touched:Connect code, the computer will begin executing the loop before it makes the connection, meaning the functions can't be called. Since neither finish nor onTouch will get called in that scenario, raceActive will never turn false, meaning the code will keep repeating into infinity. To avoid this, make sure the loop is at the very bottom of the script so that the compiler reads everything else before it begins executing the loop.

Now that we have timePassed working, turn back to the finish function and clean up your code. Replace the test print with a new message. Instead of printing "player crossed the finish line," try crafting a message that tells the player their result. Use an appropriate statement like "player finished in" and add timePassed. To combine two values in print, separate them by a comma (i.e., "player finished in", timePassed), or use the concatenation operator (..). The latter is an operator that combines multiple values into one. Note, however, that it does not automatically add space between the two values like a comma does. In that case, your statement will be: "player finished in " .. timePassed.

Additionally, you can remove the print(timePassed) code from the while loop to make your output cleaner if you want to. An easy way to do this without losing the code is to just place that line in comments.

```
local finishLine = script.Parent
local timePassed = 0
local raceActive = true

local function finish ()
    raceActive = false
    print("player finished in ".. timePassed)
end

local function onTouchFinish (otherPart)
    local character = otherPart.Parent
    local humanoid = character:FindFirstChildWhichIsA("Humanoid")
    if humanoid and raceActive == true then
        finish()
    end
end

finishLine.Touched:Connect(onTouchFinish)

while raceActive == true do
    wait (1) --wait 1 second
    timePassed = timePassed + 1 --increase timePassed by 1
    print(timePassed) --display the value of timePassed to test
end

--[[code sourced from
https://create.roblox.com/docs/education/coding-3/multiple-conditions
retrieved in March 2023]]
```

Defining Rewards

Finally, we get to the elseif. The whole point of tracking time is to create a rewards system based on how long it takes players to finish the race. Run your game and see what result you get. For example, it took me 12 seconds to beat mine.

Use this value to determine the minimum requirement for a gold medal. Since you created the course and have, by now, run it a few times, you can safely qualify this as a fast run and measure other results against it. In other words, use it as a guideline for what deserves a gold medal. For example, it took me 12 seconds, so I can set the requirement for gold at 14 seconds. Therefore, my gold medal condition will be timePassed < 14.

This will be the first condition of my elseif. Use your result to create your own gold requirement and then create alternative conditions for silver and bronze. Finally, add a message for if they failed to get either gold, silver, or bronze.

```
local function finish ()
    raceActive = false
    print("player finished in ".. timePassed)

    if timePassed < 14 then
        print("you got gold!")
    elseif 14 <= timePassed and timePassed <= 18 then
        print("you got silver!")
    elseif timePassed > 18 and timePassed < 22 then
        print("you got bronze!")
    else print("Try again!")
    end

end

--[[code adapted from
https://create.roblox.com/docs/education/coding-3/multiple-conditions
retrieved in March 2023]]
```

That's it! Run the game and test all the different rewards to make sure the game works.

7

LOOPS

WHAT ARE LOOPS?

A loop is a sequence of code that is repeated multiple times. Based on the way it is defined, loops can run a set number of times or until a condition is no longer true. Together with conditionals, loops are known as control structures, and we use them to manage the flow of execution in code. With conditionals, we determine when code should run, whereas loops let us determine how many times it runs.

Loops are a common technique used in most programming languages. You'll also find them in most online exercises and examples. Luckily, they're pretty easy to use once you understand how they work.

Lua has three main loops: for, while, and repeat. Most of what can be done with a repeat loop can also be done with a while loop. Because of this overlap, I will not cover repeat loops in this book and will instead focus on for and while loops.

WHILE LOOPS

While loops run on the basis of a condition. It works a lot like an if-statement, except that it runs more than once. With these loops, we tell the computer to keep repeating code as long as the condition remains true. The loop will only stop running once the condition becomes false.

We don't always know how many times a loop will need to run, and while loops let us base them on a condition. This means that the code will run as many times as it should without needing to know how many times it should happen. Based on the condition, it can run once, multiple times, or not at all.

While loops use the basic structure of "while [condition] do [code] end." Everything between "do" and "end" is considered part of the loop's code block and will be repeated with each iteration of the loop.

The conditions used in while loops are the same as those used in if-statements. For example, debounce ==

false, or number > 10. Regardless of what the condition is, it will return a true or false value. For the loop to run, the condition needs to be true. If it's false, the loop won't run, even if it returns false on the very first pass.

We can bypass the condition entirely to create a loop that will run independently of any condition. To do that, use "while true do."

```
while true do
    --code
end
```

Using While to Create Color Loop

Pick any of the parts in your obby and add a script named ColorChange. In it, create a variable to store the reference to the part with script.Parent. This script will use a loop to let the part continually change color every two seconds.

Once you have the variable, type "while true do" and hit enter to autofill the "end." Now, add the code that will change the part's color. If you don't remember how to do this, turn back to Chapter 4, or take a peek at the image below:

```
local changePart = script.Parent

while true do
    changePart.Color = Color3.fromRGB(255, 41, 34) --red
end
```

For the sake of functionality, add a wait between each color change. If there is no pause between the changes, the program will loop through colors faster than we can see. It's generally a good idea to include some kind of pause in loops to avoid overloading the game, especially when it comes to game-changing features like changing colors or disappearing platforms. Computers parse through code a lot faster than we as humans can. As such, it can run through an entire script in a second. Adding wait forces the program to take pauses in loops, which can greatly reduce strain on the system. You can put any value in the brackets, but for this example, it should be higher than one.

```
local changePart = script.Parent

while true do
    changePart.Color = Color3.fromRGB(255, 41, 36) --red
    wait(2)
end
```

Repeat this for however many colors you want. I want my part to cycle through the rainbow, so I'll have six color changes. Tip: Copy the two lines of code you already have and paste them for each color. You can then simply change the values in brackets.

```lua
local changePart = script.Parent

while true do
    changePart.Color = Color3.fromRGB(255, 41, 34) --red
    wait(2)
    changePart.Color = Color3.fromRGB(255, 152, 7) --orange
    wait(2)
    changePart.Color = Color3.fromRGB(255, 255, 0) --yellow
    wait(2)
    changePart.Color = Color3.fromRGB(0, 255, 0) --green
    wait(2)
    changePart.Color = Color3.fromRGB(0, 170, 255) --blue
    wait(2)
    changePart.Color = Color3.fromRGB(255, 3, 255) --purple
    wait(2)
end

--[[code adapted from
    https://create.roblox.com/docs/education/coding-4/repeating-code-with-while-loops
    retrieved in April 2023]]
```

Run the game to test if you can see all the colors you coded. If one gets skipped, check that you have a wait after each of them. If that doesn't fix it, check that the code is between the "do" and "end" of the loop.

FOR LOOPS

While loops work on the basis of a condition and use it to determine whether or not the code should be executed for each iteration. For loops, on the other hand, run a predefined number of times. It uses a control variable, or counter, with a defined starting and end point. The counter is increased with each iteration of the loop until it reaches the defined end point, which terminates the loop.

A for loop consists of three elements: namely, the control variable or counter, end point, and increment value. It is defined using the formula "for [control variable], [end point], [increment value] do." The counter acts as the determiner for the loop; it determines how many times the loop repeats. With each iteration, its value is increased or decreased with the increment value. Once it reaches the end point, the loop stops running. For example:

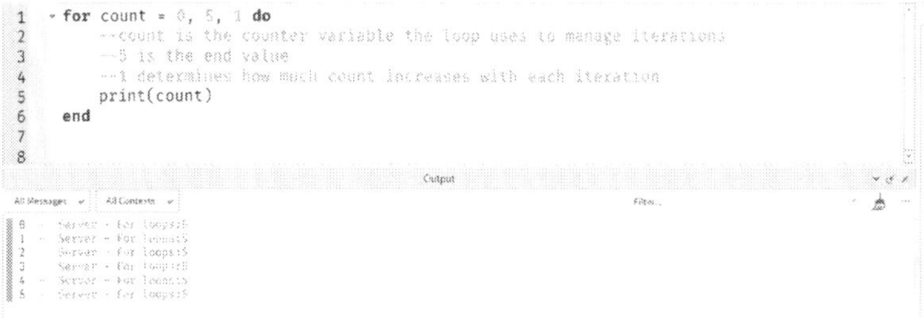

In this example, count starts with the value zero (0), which is printed in the output. Once the code has been executed, its value is increased with one, as per the increment value. On the next run of the loop, count has the value 1 and is printed as such. After this, it's increased to 2. This keeps repeating until count reaches the value 6. At this point, it has passed the end value (5), and the loop stops running.

In essence, this works the same as the conditions in if-statements and while loops. In this case, it tests whether count is less than the end point. If it is, the code is executed, and the increment value is added to the control variable (count). Each time the loop repeats, it tests count's new value against the end point.

For loops can also count backward if you use a negative value as an increment. For example:

In this example, the loop counts down from ten to zero. If we add "wait(1)" to this loop, we can turn this into an actual countdown by making it loop once per second.

For loops automatically use an increment of 1 if no other value is defined. As such, you can omit it and use "for count = 0, 10 do" and it will still add one at the end of each iteration.

For Loop Exercises

Code loops for the following exercises:

- Count up from 0 to 20.
- Count in even numbers from 0 to 20.

Do this on your own before looking at the answer below.

```
--for loop answers

--#1
for count = 0, 20, 1 do
    --code
end

--#2
for count = 0, 20, 2 do
    --code
end

--[[examples found on
    https://create.roblox.com/docs/education/coding-4/intro-to-for-loops
    retrieved in April 2023]]
```

Troubleshooting

If a for loop doesn't run the way you expect, check the following things. Check that

- the definition values are separated by commas.
- there is an appropriate wait time if the loop runs too fast.
- the starting value is less than the end point if you have a positive increment (e.g., for count = 0, 10, 1), or greater than the end point if you have a negative increment (e.g., for count = 10, 0, -1).

NESTED LOOPS

Loops can be nested, i.e., placed within each other. Each individual loop runs a certain number of times before the computer moves on to the next line of code. If one loop is contained within another, it will run in its entirety with each iteration of the parent loop.

To illustrate, look at the following example:

As you can see from the output, for each single iteration of loop A, loop B is run fully. Once loop B is finished with all its iterations, the print code in loop A is run, and then it repeats. The entirety of loop B is run for each single iteration of loop A.

Nested loops may seem abstract, but they have many applications. They can be used to repeat functional loops (like countdowns or color changes), create multiple game objects, or control the execution of other loops. Below is an example of a nested loop.

PRACTICAL EXERCISE – GLOWING LIGHTS

In this exercise, we'll create a light source that brightens and dims continually. Try the coding sections on your own before looking at the examples.

To see the light better, let's switch the project to a nighttime environment. In Explorer, find Lighting.

With it selected, turn to Properties, and find ClockTime. Set this to zero to darken the environment.

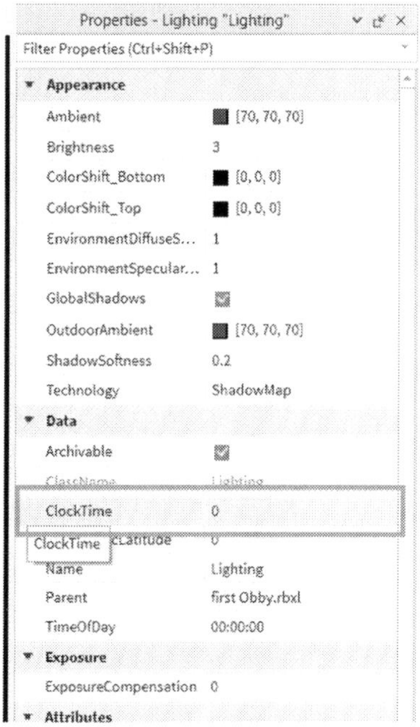

In your obby, add an object that will act as the light source and rename it Lamp. You can choose an ordinary object or find one from the Toolbox. I added a cylinder to the racetrack we made earlier. Once you have the object in a position you like, add a light part to it the same way you would add a script. You can use either PointLight or SpotLight. If you use a Toolbox model, it will likely already have one attached, but double-check.

The PointLight part has a default brightness of 1. To get the effect we want, we're going to cycle this property through different values. The value assigned to its Brightness property will act as the counter of a for loop. It will start at 0 and end at 5.

Attach a script to the Lamp part. In it, create two variables to store references to Lamp and the PointLight.

```
local lamp = script.Parent
--variable for lamp object
local light = lamp.PointLight
--variable for PointLight

```

Create two more variables. The first, brightnessChange, will store the value with which the lamp's brightness will increase. In this case, its value will be 1. The second variable, timeChange, will indicate how much time passes between each change in brightness. In other words, it will contain the value we'll use in wait statements. The reason we use a variable is to make it easier if we later want to change how much time passes.

```
local lamp = script.Parent
local light = lamp.PointLight
local brightnessChange = 1
--variable for how much the brightness changes
local timeChange = 1
--variable to indicate how much time passes

```

Glowing Loop

First, we need to create a loop that will increase the light's brightness. It will start at a brightness of 0 and end with a brightness of 5. To slowly increase it, we use a control variable called currentBrightness.

```
local lamp = script.Parent
local light = lamp.PointLight
local brightnessChange = 1
local timeChange = 1

for currentBrightness = 0, 5, brightnessChange do

end

```

In it, we set the PointLight's Brightness to current-Brightness's value and add a wait time. The time the program has to wait is the value of timeChange.

```
local lamp = script.Parent
local light = lamp.PointLight
local brightnessChange = 1
local timeChange = 1

for currentBrightness = 0, 5, brightnessChange do
    light.Brightness = currentBrightness
    wait(timeChange)
end

```

Run your game to see if the light increases in brightness.

Fading Loop

Next, we code the loop that will decrease the lamp's brightness back to 0. This loop works exactly the same as the glowing loop, only in reverse. Since we are using variables as values, you can simply copy the code for the previous loop, paste it, and change the defining values. This loop counts backward from 5 to 0, which means the control value and end value need to be adjusted. We can change the positive value of brightnessChange by putting a dash (-) in front of it to make it a negative number.

```
--to increase brightness
for currentBrightness = 0, 5, brightnessChange do
    light.Brightness = currentBrightness
    wait(timeChange)
end

--to decrease brightness
for currentBrightness = 5, 0, -brightnessChange do
    light.Brightness = currentBrightness
    wait(timeChange)
end
```

Simple as that. Run it to check that the light increases and then decreases.

Making the Loops Repeat

Finally, we need to write code to repeat these two loops continuously. Take a moment to try and find the solution on your own. Ask yourself how you can make a loop repeat itself. When you think you have the answer, look at the example below.

```
local lamp = script.Parent
local light = lamp.PointLight
local brightnessChange = 1
local timeChange = 1

while true do
    --to increase brightness
    for currentBrightness = 0, 5, brightnessChange do
        light.Brightness = currentBrightness
        wait(timeChange)
    end --of first for

    --to decrease brightness
    for currentBrightness = 5, 0, -brightnessChange do
        light.Brightness = currentBrightness
        wait(timeChange)
    end --of second for

end --of while

--[[code sourced from
    https://create.roblox.com/docs/education/coding-4/glow-lights-with-for-loops
    retrieved in April 2023]]
```

The answer is to place both loops in a while loop. On their own, each loop will run once. The first one will run until the brightness reaches 5 and then the second one will run until it's back to 0. By placing them in a while loop, we can make the program cycle through both loops repeatedly.

Run the game to test it. If it doesn't work as expected, check that both for loops are contained between the while loop's "do" and "end." You can also check that the code for each for loop is contained within their respective blocks. It sometimes helps to add a comment after each end to indicate which block it belongs to—like I did above.

This script is duplicable, so you can attach it to any object with a light source. This means you can run multiple lights on the same cycle. The code will also work for other light-giving objects like glowing crystals or celestial bodies. Because we're using variables for brightnessChange and timeChange, you can easily adjust the script to suit any circumstances by simply changing their values.

PRACTICAL EXERCISE – TIMED BRIDGE

For this exercise, we're going to use the script we already have for the button-activated bridge we made in Chapter 5. We are going to add the humanoid test to it and then set it on a timer. Once the button is pressed, it will activate a countdown. While the countdown is active, the bridge will be solid, and players can run across it. After the time has run out, the bridge should return to being transparent and impassable.

Before we get to that, add a new object to the obby to act as a display for the timer. Move and scale it into a position where players can see it as they approach and cross the bridge. Once you have it, add a SurfaceGui, and then attach a TextLabel to it.

These two items will let us display text on the block. Players can't access the output window and, as such, can't see any messages displayed there. Thus, we need to display things we want players to see in some other way.

If you can't immediately see the TextLabel on the block, don't panic. They start out pretty small and don't always attach where you expect them to. Select the SurfaceGui and find its Face property.

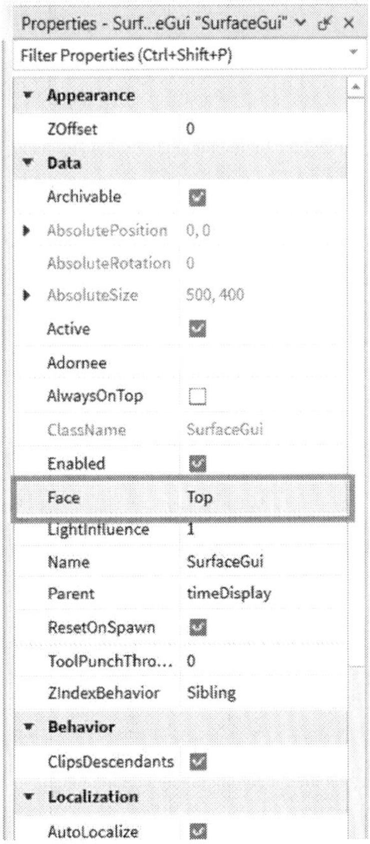

Changing this affects where the TextLabel is placed on the block. I had to move it to Top, but yours might be different depending on how it's been moved. Once you have it on the right face, it'll look like this:

Now we have to resize it. Select TextLabel in Explorer and go to its Size property. Under it, there are two subproperties, X and Y. For both, set their Scale to 1 and Offset to 0. This centers the text on the block. Next, scroll down to TextScaled. Enable this to automatically scale the text to the size of the block. Finally, find Text and delete what's in it.

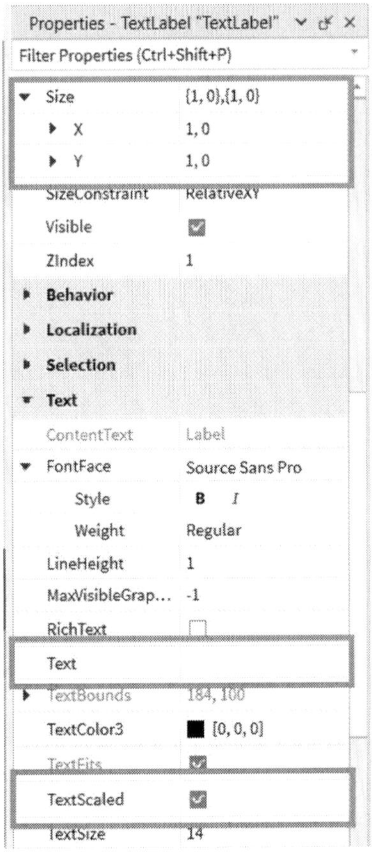

Changing the Script

Since we already have code managing the button's Touched event, we'll simply add onto it. You can, of course, start over from scratch if you want to. This is where we left off in this script:

```
local button = script.Parent
local bridge = game.Workspace.Bridge.bridge
local debounce = false

local function onButtonPress ()
    if debounce == false then
        debounce = true
        button.Color = Color3.fromRGB(0, 255, 0)
        bridge.Transparency = 0
        bridge.CanCollide = true
        print("button pressed, bridge available")
    end
end

button.Touched:Connect(onButtonPress)
```

What we need to do is

1. create variables to reference the block's textlabel and the maximum timer value (this will determine how long the bridge stays up).
2. include a humanoid condition to test for players touching the button.
3. create a new function called startTimer and move the code from the onButtonPress if-statement to it. In the if-statement, call startTimer.
4. use a loop to create a timer that counts down from the maximum timer value to 0.
5. create code that reverts the bridge to impassable once the time runs out.

These are all things you've done before. Try doing them yourself before looking at the answer. Below, I'll walk you through the code and the steps involved.

First, create a variable for the display text, called timerText. To display the countdown, we need to change the Text property of the TextLabel. To access this property, we'll have to use the TextLabel's whole path. While we're up here, let's also create the variable to store how long the bridge will stay traversable. My bridge is pretty short, so 5 seconds will be enough time to cross it. Thus, timerDuration = 5.

```
local button = script.Parent
local bridge = game.Workspace.Bridge.bridge
local timerText = game.Workspace.Bridge.timeDisplay.SurfaceGui.TextLabel
local timerDuration = 5
local debounce = false

```

Second, we need to add code to make the button test whether a player touched it. Simply add the variables for character and humanoid to the existing function and add the condition to the if-statement. I also added otherPart as a parameter since we reference it for the character variable's initialization.

```

local function onButtonPress (otherPart)
    local character = otherPart.Parent
    local humanoid = character:FindFirstChildWhichIsA("Humanoid")

    if humanoid and debounce == false then
        debounce = true
        button.Color = Color3.fromRGB(0, 255, 0)
        bridge.Transparency = 0
        bridge.CanCollide = true
        print("button pressed, bridge available")
    end
end

```

Third, create a new function called startTimer. Cut the code from the if-statement in onButtonPress and paste it into startTimer. Call this new function in the if-statement.

```
local function startTimer ()
    debounce = true
    button.Color = Color3.fromRGB(0, 255, 0)
    bridge.Transparency = 0
    bridge.CanCollide = true
    print("button pressed, bridge available")
end

local function onButtonPress (otherPart)
    local character = otherPart.Parent
    local humanoid = character:FindFirstChildWhichIsA("Humanoid")

    if humanoid and debounce == false then
        startTimer()
    end
end

button.Touched:Connect(onButtonPress)
```

Play the game to test that the bridge button still works.

Create a Timer

This timer will manage how long the bridge is open. While the timer is active, the player can walk across the bridge. Once the time runs out, the bridge becomes impassable again. To do this, we need a for loop that will count down from timerDuration to zero. If you haven't yet created the loop on your own, try. In the loop block, change the TextLabel's Text property to reflect the value of the counter used in the loop. Add a wait(1) to make the loop run once per second.

```
local function startTimer ()
    debounce = true
    button.Color = Color3.fromRGB(0, 255, 0)
    bridge.Transparency = 0
    bridge.CanCollide = true
    print("button pressed, bridge available")

    for count = timerDuration, 0, -1 do
        timerText.Text = count
        wait(1)
    end
end
```

Run your game to check that the bridge is only solid while the timer is running. If it isn't, check that all the code is where it should be, that everything is spelled correctly, and that the parts are assigned to the correct variables.

8

ARRAYS AND DICTIONARIES

We've covered tables a little in a previous chapter. Tables are collections of related data gathered in one object. Unlike regular variables, they do not just store a single value. Instead, they contain multiple values, each with its own unique identifier.

In Lua, there are two types of tables: namely, arrays and dictionaries.

ARRAYS

Arrays are a common feature of most programming languages. They also have tons of applications; people use them in data management, game development, general-purpose programming, system engineering, and more. They're a very common programming technique and being able to work with them is a useful skill.

An array is declared with a name like any other code object. It can also be given local scope or left as global. Its values are listed in curly brackets (i.e., {...}) and separated by commas. For example:

```
local testArray = {"one", "two", "three", "four", "five"}
```

Arrays are tables that store ordered lists. Values are listed in a specific order and given a corresponding numerical index number based on the order in which they are listed. The first entry is stored at index 1, the second at index 2, and so on. Above, value "one" is linked to 1, "two" to 2, "three" to 3, and so on. Unlike many other languages, indexes in Lua start at 1 and not 0 (zero).

Lua arrays don't have a fixed length. Length refers to the number of elements contained in an array, elements meaning the items contained within it. In Lua, length is determined automatically by the number of elements. If you add or remove items, the length is adjusted. This means that arrays can grow and shrink as needed. If an array has no items, it is given the value nil.

To access specific values in an array, you need to reference the name of the array, and then the index number of the value you're looking for. The index is always placed in square brackets (i.e., [...]). For example, testArray[2].

To access elements of the array, we use a for loop to cycle through all the available indexes. The control variable represents the value of the index. For example, if I wanted to print all elements of testArray, I'd use the following code:

```
local testArray = {"one", "two", "three", "four", "five"}

for k = 1, 5, 1 do
    print(testArray[k])
end
```

```
one - Server - Arrays:5
two - Server - Arrays:5
three - Server - Arrays:5
four - Server - Arrays:5
five - Server - Arrays:5
```

You'll notice that I use the variable k as a control. This is mostly for the sake of habit and convenience. It's common to use variable names like k or i for counters since they're unspecific and unlikely to be used in any other circumstances. Since I always use k for array loops, I won't ever name any other variable k and can thus immediately tell what this loop is for.

In this example, I use 5 as the end value. Since you won't always know the length of the array, it's better to use #arrayName instead. Coding “for k = 1, #testArray, 1 do” will have the same result but makes provision for if the array grows or shrinks.

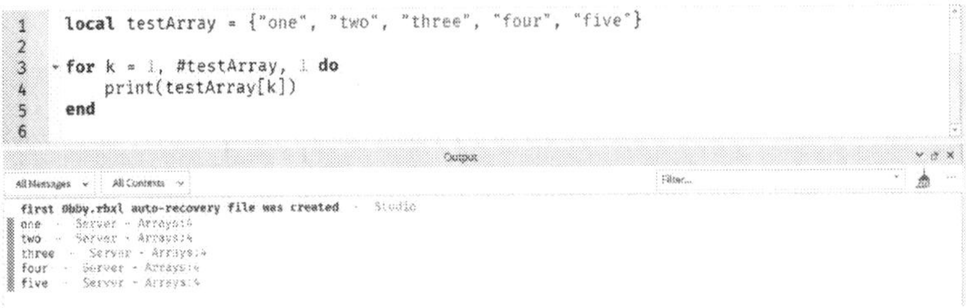

PRACTICAL EXERCISE USING ARRAYS

In your obby, create a segmented path consisting of multiple blocks. Use at least three parts and line them up to create a path. These parts will disappear separately one after the other and then reappear. First, create a folder called disappearingPath. In it, create a script and then another folder named Parts. The subfolder will contain the various parts that form the path.

Next, create the individual parts. I’d recommend making one, transforming it into what you want, and then duplicating it for the others. Rename them something like pathPart1, pathPart2, and pathPart3. Make sure that they are in the Parts folder.

Now create variables in the script to reference these folders.

```
local path = script.Parent
local partsFolder = path.Parts

```

Define an array and reference each of the path parts in it. Place each item on a separate line to make it easier to read and remember to separate them with commas. Your path can include as many parts as you want, just make sure to reference each part in the array. If, for example, you have five path parts, you need five array elements.

```

local partsArray = {
    partsFolder.pathPart1,
    partsFolder.pathPart2,
    partsFolder.pathPart3
}

```

To run through the different parts and make them disappear, we use a loop. This will let us make them disappear one at a time with a pause in between. First, set up the loop to run from 1 to #partsArray. Next, declare a variable outside the loop to represent how long the game should pause between each disappearance. For testing purposes, make this time short, one or two seconds. You can change this later to give players enough time to cross the path.

In the loop, add code to make the game wait. This should be the first line of the loop since we want to delay the disappearance of the first block.

```
local disappearTime = 2

for k = 1, #partsArray, 1 do
    wait(disappearTime)
end
```

Next, we want a variable to contain a reference to the part we're managing. Create a local variable called whichPart in the loop and assign it the value partsArray[k]. In this case, k represents the index value of each array element.

```
local disappearTime = 2

for k = 1, #partsArray, 1 do
    wait(disappearTime)
    local whichPart = partsArray[k]
end
```

We'll use whichPart to access each part's properties. Do you remember how we made the button-activated bridge vanish? Use that example to write the code to make whichPart disappear. If you can't remember, turn back to the bridge examples from Chapter 5 or Chapter 7. Finally, add a suitable display message to test the loop.

```
for k = 1, #partsArray, 1 do
    wait(disappearTime)
    local whichPart = partsArray[k]
    whichPart.CanCollide = false
    whichPart.Transparency = 1
    print("Part #", k, "has disappeared")
end
```

Run the game and check that the parts vanish one after the other. It takes time to load into the game, and by the time you spawn in, the path could already be gone. If this happens, increase the value of disappearTime.

If it doesn't work, check that you reference the correct parts in the array, that values in it are separated by commas, and that you have the correct values in the for loop declaration.

As is, the parts only disappear once at the start of the game and then they remain gone, meaning players can't get across at all. To fix this, let's add another loop to make them reappear. To do this, copy the existing loop and paste it below the first. Leave the loop declaration as is and change the whichPart properties to make the objects visible again. You can choose to leave the wait period to make them reappear in sequence or remove it to make them reappear all at once. If you remove the wait from the second loop, add a wait between the loops to create a delay between the last disappearance and the path's reappearance.

```
    wait(disappearTime)

    for k = 1, #partsArray, 1 do
        local whichPart = partsArray[k]
        whichPart.CanCollide = true
        whichPart.Transparency = 0
        print("Part #", k, "has reappeared")
    end

```

Finally, place both loops in a while loop. Without the while loop, the parts will disappear and then reappear permanently. For it to be a continuous cycle, the loops should repeat. Run the game and test that it works. Once it does, you can remove the print code since we only use it to test that the loops work as intended.

```
local path = script.Parent
local partsFolder = path.Parts

local partsArray = {
    partsFolder.pathPart1,
    partsFolder.pathPart2,
    partsFolder.pathPart3
}

local disappearTime = 2

while true do
    for k = 1, #partsArray, 1 do --disappear loop
        wait(disappearTime)
        local whichPart = partsArray[k]
        whichPart.CanCollide = false
        whichPart.Transparency = 1
    end

    wait(disappearTime)

    for k = 1, #partsArray, 1 do --reappear loop
        local whichPart = partsArray[k]
        whichPart.CanCollide = true
        whichPart.Transparency = 0
    end
end
--[[code adapted from https://create.roblox.com/docs/education/coding-5/loops-and-arrays
    retrieved in April 2023]]
```

MODIFYING ARRAYS

Arrays aren't static; their values can still change after they've been declared. You can change the values assigned to elements, add new entries, and remove existing items. These are useful tricks to know since we often use arrays for inventory systems and when managing player data.

Adding Elements

The simplest way to add new entries is to add another line in the array declaration. Since this isn't always possible, you can also use code outside the definition. To do this, use "table.insert(...)." This function takes two parameters, the name of the array and then the value you want to assign to it. This will assign that value to the next available index number.

```lua
local modifyArray = { }

table.insert(modifyArray, "one")
table.insert(modifyArray, "two")
table.insert(modifyArray, "three")

for k = 1, #modifyArray,1 do
    print(modifyArray[k])
end
```

```
one - Server - Arrays 2:8
two - Server - Arrays 2:8
three - Server - Arrays 2:8
```

Above, I declared an empty array and then used table.insert to add three new elements. As you can see, this array displays exactly the same as the other example despite it being initialized differently. You can also use this to add onto arrays with preexisting values.

```
local modifyArray = {"one", "two", "three"}

table.insert(modifyArray, "four")
table.insert(modifyArray, "five")
table.insert(modifyArray, "six")

for k = 1, #modifyArray,1 do
    print(modifyArray[k])
end
```

```
Output
All Messages    5 Contexts    Filter...
one - Server - Arrays 2:8
two - Server - Arrays 2:8
three - Server - Arrays 2:8
four - Server - Arrays 2:8
five - Server - Arrays 2:8
six - Server - Arrays 2:8
```

Remove Elements

There's also a function to remove items. For this, use table.remove to delete the last entry in an array. Unlike its counterpart, it only takes the array name as a parameter, i.e., table.remove(modifyArray). Let's add this to modifyArray.

```
local modifyArray = {"one", "two", "three"}

table.insert(modifyArray, "four")
table.insert(modifyArray, "five")
table.insert(modifyArray, "six")

table.remove(modifyArray)

for k = 1, #modifyArray,1 do
    print(modifyArray[k])
end
```

```
Output
All Messages    5 Contexts    Filter...
one - Server - Arrays 2:10
two - Server - Arrays 2:10
three - Server - Arrays 2:10
four - Server - Arrays 2:10
five - Server - Arrays 2:10
```

As you can see, the last element we inserted was removed and is thus missing from the output.

You can also remove items per their index by adding them as a second parameter. If I wanted to remove the third element from modifyArray, I would use table.remove(modifyArray, 3).

```lua
local modifyArray = {"one", "two", "three"}

table.insert(modifyArray, "four")
table.insert(modifyArray, "five")
table.insert(modifyArray, "six")

table.remove(modifyArray, 3)

for k = 1, #modifyArray,1 do
    print(modifyArray[k])
end
```

```
Output
All Messages    5 Contexts    Filter...
one - Server - Arrays 2:10
two - Server - Arrays 2:10
four - Server - Arrays 2:10
five - Server - Arrays 2:10
six - Server - Arrays 2:10
```

Note that this affects the index numbers of the rest of the array. Arrays are ordered lists, and indexes follow an ordinal pattern. If I display the array with its indexes, you'll see that modifyArray[3] now has the value "four" instead of "three" as it was defined.

```lua
local modifyArray = {"one", "two", "three"}

table.insert(modifyArray, "four")
table.insert(modifyArray, "five")
table.insert(modifyArray, "six")

table.remove(modifyArray, 3)

for k = 1, #modifyArray,1 do
    print(k, modifyArray[k])
end
```

```
Output
All Messages    5 Contexts    Filter...
1 one - Server - Arrays 2:10
2 two - Server - Arrays 2:10
3 four - Server - Arrays 2:10
4 five - Server - Arrays 2:10
5 six - Server - Arrays 2:10
```

Searching for a Value

You can also search through the elements of an array to find a specific element. We can use a for loop to cycle through the indexes and a conditional to test each value against what we're looking for. Create a function with the name of the array and value you're searching for as parameters. In it, create the for loop.

```
local searchArray = {"one", "two", "three", "four", "five", "six"}

local function findValue(arrayName, searchValue)
    for k = 1, #arrayName, 1 do

    end
end

```

Here, searchValue contains the value we're looking for, and each array value should be compared to it via a conditional. In this case, the condition will be "if searchArray[k] == searchValue." If the condition succeeds (i.e., the values match), the function returns the index number of the element.

```
local searchArray = {"one", "two", "three", "four", "five", "six"}

local function findValue(arrayName, searchValue)
    for k = 1, #arrayName, 1 do
        if arrayName[k] == searchValue then
            return k
        end --of if
    end --of for
end --of function

```

To test the function, create a variable called valueFound. For its initialization, call the function and give it the necessary arguments. Then, print valueFound with an appropriate message.

```lua
local searchArray = {"one", "two", "three", "four", "five", "six"}

local function findValue(arrayName, searchValue)
    for k = 1, #arrayName, 1 do
        if arrayName[k] == searchValue then
            return k
        end --of if
    end --of for
end --of function

local valueFound = findValue(searchArray, "two")

print("value found at index", valueFound)
```

Output

```
All Messages  5 Contexts  Filter...
value found at index 2 - Server - Arrays 2:13
```

The reason why we might search an array is to find specific elements so that we can use, display, or remove them. For example, let's remove the value we found. Above, the function searched for "two" and found it at index 2. To remove it, use the valueFound variable as a parameter in table.remove.

```lua
local searchArray = {"one", "two", "three", "four", "five", "six"}

local function findValue(arrayName, searchValue)
    for k = 1, #arrayName, 1 do
        if arrayName[k] == searchValue then
            return k
        end --of if
    end --of for
end --of function

local valueFound = findValue(searchArray, "two")

print("value found at index", valueFound)

table.remove(searchArray, valueFound)

for k = 1, #searchArray,1 do
    print(searchArray[k])
end
```

Output

```
All Messages  5 Contexts  Filter...
value found at index 2 - Server - Arrays 2:13
one - Server - Arrays 2:18
three - Server - Arrays 2:18
four - Server - Arrays 2:18
five - Server - Arrays 2:18
six - Server - Arrays 2:18
```

Simplify the code by moving the remove statement inside the loop and deleting valueFound. This makes code more effective since it will remove all elements with that value and not just the first one it finds.

```
local searchArray = {"one", "two", "three", "four", "five", "two", "six"}

for k = 1, #searchArray, 1 do
    if searchArray[k] == "two" then
        print("value found at index", k)
        table.remove(searchArray, k)
    end --of if
end --of for

for k = 1, #searchArray,1 do
    print(searchArray[k])
end

--[[code adapted from
    https://create.roblox.com/docs/education/coding-5/making-changes-to-arrays
    retrieved in April 2023]]
```

```
Output
All Messages    5 Contexts    Filter...
value found at index 2  -  Server - Arrays 2:5
value found at index 5  -  Server - Arrays 2:5
one  -  Server - Arrays 2:11
three  -  Server - Arrays 2:11
four  -  Server - Arrays 2:11
five  -  Server - Arrays 2:11
six  -  Server - Arrays 2:11
```

Above, I added an additional element with the value "two" into the array, and the function removed both instances.

Arrays aren't always as simple as this in practice. These examples use simplified objects to illustrate the basics. However, the logic remains the same regardless of how complex the array or project is. Keep this in mind for when your projects start growing in complexity.

EXTRA PRACTICE

For some extra practice, create an NPC and post them somewhere in your obby. When you make them (or choose them from the Toolbox) make sure they have a ClickDetector child.

This NPC will react to player clicks with dialogue. The dialogue it responds with will be stored in an array called dialogueArray. To make the NPC speak, use the Chat method stored in the Chat service. If you call this method, it will ask you for two parameters. The first will refer to the object that speaks, and the second will refer to what it says. Use a combination of functions, variables, and array management to set up an array that contains a few different sentences the NPC can cycle through.

The answer is below but try this on your own first.

```
local Chat = game:GetService("Chat")

local npc = script.Parent
local characterParts = npc.CharacterParts
local head = characterParts.Head
local clickDetector = npc.ClickDetector

--Add table below
local dialogueArray= {"Hi!", "Do I know you?", "How are you?"}
local arrayIndex = 2 --value of index number

local function speak()
    local dialogue = dialogueArray[arrayIndex]
    Chat:Chat(head, dialogue)
    arrayIndex = arrayIndex + 1
end

clickDetector.MouseClick:Connect(speak)

--[[code sourced form https://create.roblox.com/docs/education/coding-5/intro-to-arrays#creating-the-talking-character
    retrieved in April 2023]]
```

DICTIONARIES

The second type of table you'll encounter is a dictionary. Dictionaries are similar to arrays in that they store multiple values within one object. However, here, values are stored in relation to a key instead of a sequential index number. Where arrays act as ordered lists, dictionaries label values.

Each entry has a key and assigned value. The key acts similar to indexes in that it differentiate values from other entries. The difference is that keys aren't limited to sequential numbers. While you can add keys of various data types, it's better to stick to one. This makes dictionaries easier to manage and manipulate. Each key needs to be unique so it can act as an identifier. In other words, you cannot have two keys with the same name in the same dictionary.

Where arrays can be used to store and manipulate ordered lists, dictionaries are better suited to more complex structures like inventory systems or item stats.

Dictionaries are defined the same way arrays are, with a name, "=" and curly brackets. Each entry is placed on a new line with the formula key = value. Each item is separated by a comma. For example:

```
local cutlass = {
    name = "Cutlass",
    description = "A pirate's weapon",
    atk = 17,
    def = 3,
    spd = 2,
    critDamage = 0.1
}

```

In this example, the dictionary contains data related to a weapon. To use any of these values, we need to call the item by the name of the dictionary and the key; e.g., cutlass["atk"].

```
local cutlass = {
    name = "Cutlass",
    description = "A pirate's weapon",
    atk = 17,
    def = 3,
    spd = 2,
    critDamage = 0.1
}

print(cutlass["atk"])
```

Modifying Dictionaries

You can modify a dictionary by referencing the table and key and then assigning a new value to it. This overrides the previous value. For example:

```
local cutlass = {
    name = "Cutlass",
    description = "A pirate's weapon",
    atk = 17,
    def = 3,
    spd = 2,
    critDamage = 0.1
}

cutlass["atk"] = 25

print(cutlass["atk"])
```

To create a new entry, simply reference a new key, and then assign it a value. For example:

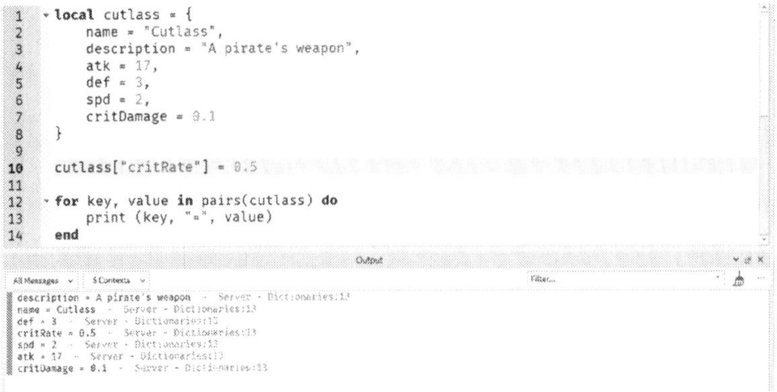

Here you can see that I added a new item called critRate. When the dictionary is displayed, you can see that the new item is included. If you're wondering about the loop I used to display it, we generally use a function called pairs to manipulate dictionaries. Unlike arrays, dictionaries don't have sequential keys we can use as a counter. Instead, we use pairs to loop through each key-value pair contained in the table.

Removing items from a dictionary is as simple as adding them. Simply change the value of the item you want to remove to nil. For example, if I change cutlass["description"] to have the value nil, it will be removed from the dictionary.

```lua
local cutlass = {
    name = "Cutlass",
    description = "A pirate's weapon",
    atk = 17,
    def = 3,
    spd = 2,
    critDamage = 0.1
}

cutlass["description"] = nil

for key, value in pairs(cutlass) do
    print (key, "=", value)
end
```

```
Output
All Messages    5 Contexts    Filter...
name = Cutlass    Server - Dictionaries:13
def = 3  -  Server - Dictionaries:13
spd = 2  -  Server - Dictionaries:13
atk = 17  -  Server - Dictionaries:13
critDamage = 0.1    Server - Dictionaries:13
```

Dictionaries and Other Variables

You can use preexisting variables to supply data to a table. Say you want to use the value of a predefined variable as the key in a dictionary. Think, for example, of scenarios where you want to use the name of a player or value that will be calculated in a function. In that case, you can use the variable as the key. Instead of the key being the name of the variable, it will instead be its value. For example:

```lua
local cutlass = {
    name = "Cutlass",
    description = "A pirate's weapon",
    atk = 17,
    def = 3,
    spd = 2,
    critDamage = 0.1,
}

local newKey = "critRate" --variable containing the new key
cutlass[newKey] = 0.5 --new entry using the variable

for key, value in pairs(cutlass) do
    print (key, "=", value)
end
```

```
Output
All Messages    5 Contexts    Filter...
description = A pirate's weapon  -  Server - Dictionaries:14
name = Cutlass  -  Server - Dictionaries:14
def = 3    Server - Dictionaries:14
critRate = 0.5  -  Server - Dictionaries:14
spd = 2  -  Server - Dictionaries:14
atk = 17  -  Server - Dictionaries:14
critDamage = 0.1  -  Server - Dictionaries:14
```

In this example, you can see that I use newKey to create a key called "critRate." When the table is displayed, it displays "critRate" and not newKey.

This example is somewhat abstract since this isn't really a situation in which you would use a variable. However, you can use the same logic to reference things like players' names retrieved from events or objects instanced through code.

PAIRS AND IPAIRS

Pairs and ipairs are built-in functions you can use to work with dictionaries and arrays when you want to manipulate their data. Both are used with a for loop. In this case, the for loop does not use a control, end value, or increment. Instead, it uses the key or index and their corresponding values along with the table name.

Pairs and Dictionaries

When working with dictionaries, we use the function pairs. This lets us access table keys and their corresponding values without needing to specify which entry we're working with. It basically lets us work with each entry as a pair. Pairs is used with the following code: for key, value in pairs(dictionaryName) do. For example, in "atk = 17," atk is the key, and 17 is the value.

This is then stored in the key and value variables to be used however needed.

To illustrate, let's create a quick script that organizes players into a dictionary based on assigned colors. Use any colors or names to create a few entries. Then use a for loop and pairs to display both the name and color.

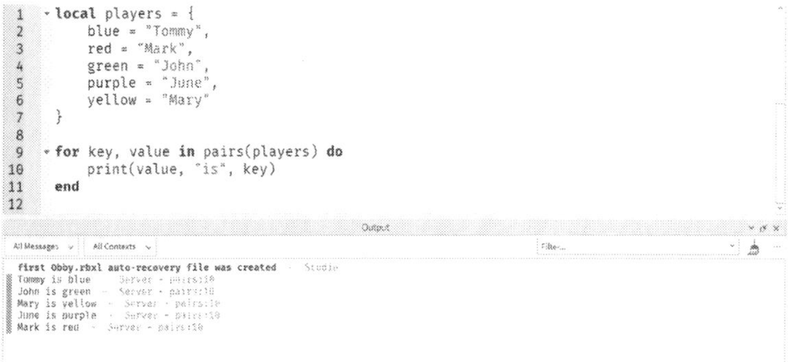

Note that you don't have to use "key" and "value" with this loop. You can give them any name you want, like assignedColor and playerName. These are just temporary variables that store the keys and values of each item in the dictionary. The code "for color, name in pairs(players) do" will work just as well as the above example.

Ipairs and Arrays

When working with arrays, there are two ways you can go about it. You can use a control variable that represents the index number, or you can use ipairs. Ipairs lets us link the value to the index number and work with them as a pair. You use it with a for loop and declare it with the code "for index, value in ipairs(arrayName) do."

This is a great alternative to normal for loops for cases where the item value should be tied to the index. If, for example, your array represents a leaderboard, the index values have meaning beyond just indicating the location of the value. In that case, the value of the index number has a meaning.

For example, let's assume the following array contains the names of players sorted by their highest score. Index 1 represents the player with the highest score while index 5 contains the name of the one with the lowest score. Placed in an ipairs loop, we can individually reference both values independently to create a display message.

```
local leaderboard = {
    "Ali",
    "May",
    "Cammy",
    "Ben",
    "Alex"
}

for rank, name in ipairs(leaderboard) do
    print("#"..rank.." is ".. name)
end

--[[code adpated from
    https://create.roblox.com/docs/education/coding-5/pairs-and-ipairs
    retrieved in April 2023]]
```

```
#1 is Ali - Server - ipairs:10
#2 is May - Server - ipairs:10
#3 is Cammy - Server - ipairs:10
#4 is Ben - Server - ipairs:10
#5 is Alex - Server - ipairs:10
```

Like above, the names you use to represent the index and value don't matter. You can use specific descriptors like above or general words like index and value.

PRACTICAL EXERCISE

Let's combine arrays and dictionaries into one exercise. Here, we are going to create a simplified soup simulator. The game will have a dictionary that stores potential ingredients. The player will select a few, and those will be added into a soup. The soup will be represented by an array that will store the chosen ingredients. Finally, we will display the soup to the player using the array.

For now, we are only going to make the code for this simulator without creating the game itself. As always, try this on your own first before looking at the walkthrough of the answer below. Here is a list of the things you'll need to do:

- Create an ingredients dictionary. The key for each item is the name of the ingredient, and the value represents whether it is added to the soup. All items should start off as false. They become true once they've been chosen by a player.

- Make a loop to search through the items to find any with the value true. The ones that are true should be added into an array.
- Find a way to test whether the array has any elements. If it does, display those elements as the chosen ingredients; if it doesn't, display an appropriate message.

First, create a dictionary of ingredients. This dictionary acts as a menu from which players can choose. Add as many items as you want but try to add at least five. The name of the ingredient is the key, and all the values are false. You can also create an empty array called inSoup.

```
local ingredients = {
    potato = false,
    tomato = false,
    kale = false,
    chicken = false,
    rice = false,
    beef = false,
    beans = false,
    peas = false,
}

local inSoup = {}
```

Second, code a loop that will cycle through all these items. I use the variables menuChoice and value to contain the key and value of each item. In this loop, set up a conditional that will test whether any of the values are true. You can use the condition "if value then" to do this. Any item with the value false will fail this condition. Create code to sort the items that succeed into the inSoup array using table.insert.

```
local ingredients = {
    potato = false,
    tomato = false,
    kale = false,
    chicken = false,
    rice = false,
    beef = false,
    beans = false,
    peas = false,
}

local inSoup = {}

for menuChoice, value in pairs(ingredients) do
    if value then
        table.insert(inSoup, menuChoice)
    end
end
```

This code will test the value of each item and then store the key to the array. For example, if tomato was chosen and thus true, it would pass the conditional. Only "tomato" will be inserted into the array.

Thirdly, we need to code appropriate responses. If this was an actual game, it would need to know if any ingredients were chosen to determine how to react. If something is chosen, the game has to respond by making soup with the chosen ingredients. If nothing was chosen, there shouldn't be any soup.

In our case, if items were selected, they will be displayed in the output. If nothing was chosen, an alternative message should be displayed instead. To test if ingredients were selected, we have to see whether the array has any entries. Remember, items will only be added to the array if they are true. If none are, the array will be empty. So how do we test this? With an if-statement to test whether the array's length is more than zero with "if #array > 0 then."

```
for menuChoice, value in pairs(ingredients) do
    if value then
        table.insert(inSoup, menuChoice)
    end
end


if #inSoup > 0 then
    print("Your soup contains:")
    for itemNumber, chosen in ipairs(inSoup) do
        print(chosen)
    end
else print("Nothing was chosen, aren't you hungry?")
end

--[[code adapted from
    https://create.roblox.com/docs/education/coding-5/pairs-and-ipairs
    retrieved in April 2023]]
```

To test whether the code works, make one or two of the ingredients true and hit play. If it works, those ingredients will be displayed.

For example, here's what happens when I run it with all ingredients false:

```
local ingredients = {
    potato = false,
    tomato = false,
    kale = false,
    chicken = false,
    rice = false,
    beef = false,
    beans = false,
    peas = false
}
```

```
Output
All Messages   5 Contexts   Filter...
Nothing was chosen, aren't you hungry?  -  Server - Soup simulator:26
```

Here's what happens if some are true:

Don't worry if the items don't print in the same order they're listed in the table. While arrays are handled sequentially, dictionaries aren't. This means that items aren't handled in the order you might expect.

If your code doesn't work, check that all the names were typed correctly in the loop and conditional, that lines of code are where they should be, and that the final if-statement comes after the for loop.

Additional Challenges

If you want to get more out of this exercise, try making this into an actual game by adding the following features:

- Create visual items for each ingredient and use their Touched to turn the values true.

- Add an NPC or display object that will show the output message to a player.
- Turn the game around entirely and add dictionaries that store specific recipes. Use the code logic to make the player the chef who has to choose ingredients based on those recipes.

NEXT UP

Now that we've covered the basics of coding, we're going to put it into practice. In the next two chapters, you're going to build two different experiences: an adventure game and a battle royale. These two games will reinforce different coding concepts as well as teach you different techniques to build game environments.

9

BUILD AN ADVENTURE GAME

PROJECT PLANNING

Planning is the first and most important step of any project. This is called pre-production and involves creating a game design document where you explore your ideas in more detail. This document doesn't have to be long and complicated, and you can do it in a Word editor or on a piece of paper.

This document should contain the following:

- the concept of the game
- what players will do when playing
- the game loop
- basic mechanics

- description of the setting (the world the game takes place in)
- a rough sketch of the map and environment
- any items or tools added to the game
- possible upgrades for equipment.

This game is an adventure game. Its objective is to make players explore a world to find specific objects. It features a fairly simple game loop or premise: Players explore, harvest items, sell them, and upgrade their gear. Then, they can return to exploring.

In this project, we'll

- make a map.
- code a leaderboard.
- create items to harvest and a tool to use.
- provide a selling feature.
- create an upgrade system.

CREATE A MAP

Make a rough sketch of the map. Plan where players will spawn, where items can be harvested and sold, and an upgrade station. You can also map out environment details like trees, water, mountains, and paths. Once you have that, create a new Roblox project with the Flat Terrain template.

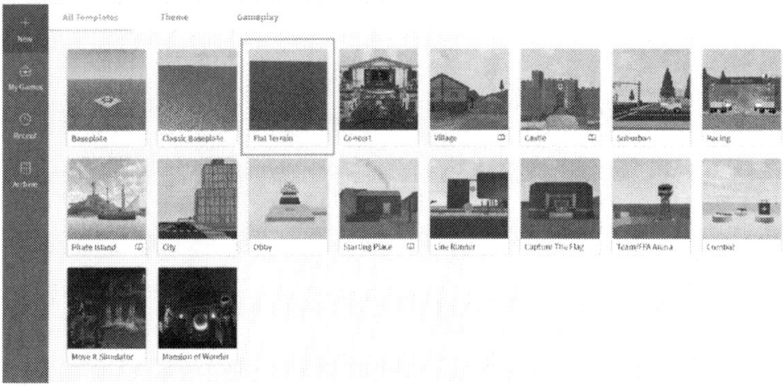

For this project, we are going to create the world from scratch using the Terrain Editor. Once you have the project ready, open the Terrain Editor and click on Edit. There you'll see these tools:

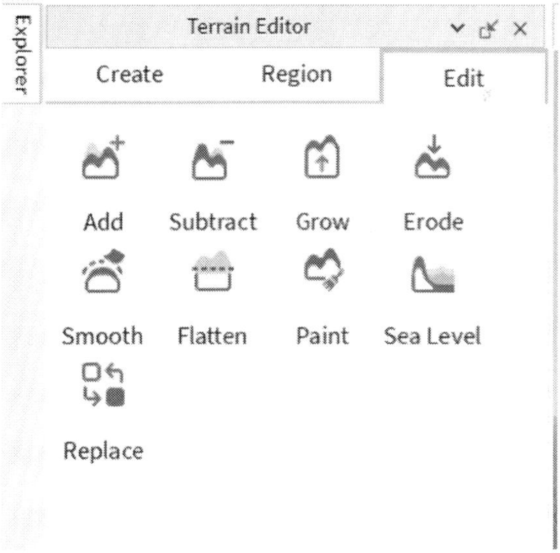

First, use Paint to create the basic layout of your map. Keep your planning sketch nearby for reference. Experiment with different areas, materials, and brushes. Remember to save regularly and view your project from different angles.

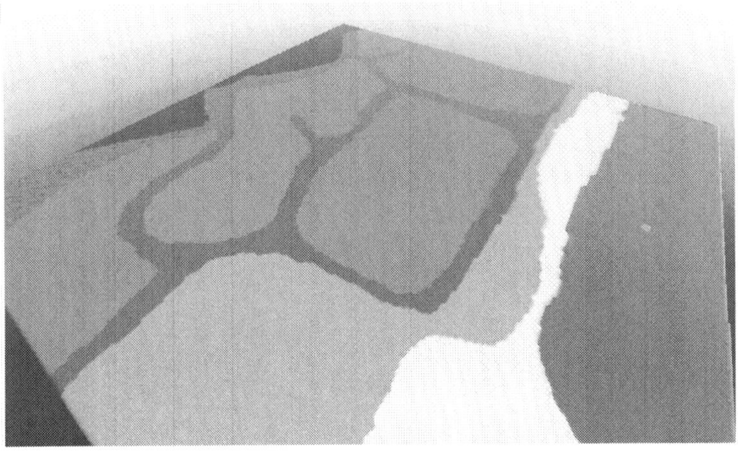

Next, use the other tools to add variety to the environment. Add lets you build onto the terrain to create mountains and hills. Subtract lets you cut out sections of the terrain to create valleys and dips. Other tools like Smooth and Flatten can help you refine these shapes while Grow and Erode can help you add more dimension. Take this opportunity to play around with the Terrain Editor. See what you can accomplish and build. Add mountains, dig trenches for rivers, erode areas to create bumpier terrain, etc.

To illustrate, I added some mountains and a river to the project.

You can go ahead and add a SpawnLocation. Don't worry about adding any other decorations or items just yet.

CODE A LEADERBOARD

Roblox automatically creates a leaderboard in every experience. At default, it only displays the names of the players who join. Since this is an automatic feature, we can use it to also display player stats. We do this first to make playtesting other game mechanics easier.

Create a script in ServerScriptService and name it PlayerSetup. Here, we'll instance a folder that will be attached to each player and then store three variables in that folder to represent three stats. We'll use the PlayerAdded event to do this.

In the script, create a function to connect to the event. It will take the parameter player. In it, create a variable called leaderstats. Its value is an instance of the type "Folder." Use the properties .Name and .Parent to give it the name "leaderstats" and set its parent as player. It's important that its name be "leaderstats" since this will let us use it for the leaderboard.

```
local function onPlayerJoin(player)
    local leaderstats = Instance.new("Folder")
    leaderstats.Name = "leaderstats"
    leaderstats.Parent = player
end

```

Our leaderboard will track three stats:

- Gold: represents how much money the player has available
- Items: how many items are in their possession
- Spaces: the amount of inventory space they have

Each of these variables will be instances of the type "IntValue." IntValues are just number variables, but this method lets us attach them to each player as an object.

Declare a new variable called "gold" in the function and initialize it with Instance.new("IntValue"). Change its

.Name to "Gold." To give it a value, use its .Value property and set it to 0. Finally, make it a child of the leaderstats folder.

```
    local gold = Instance.new("IntValue")
    gold.Name = "Gold"
    gold.Value = 0
    gold.Parent = leaderstats
    --adding a Gold section to the leaderboard
end
```

Do the same thing for the other two variables (items and spaces). Copy and paste this code, and change the values as needed. For spaces, assign the value 2.

```
local function onPlayerJoin(player)
    local leaderstats = Instance.new("Folder")
    leaderstats.Name = "leaderstats"
    leaderstats.Parent = player
    --adding the player to the leaderboard

    --adding sections into the leaderboard to display Gold, Items, and Spaces
    local gold = Instance.new("IntValue")
    gold.Name = "Gold"
    gold.Value = 0
    gold.Parent = leaderstats

    local items = Instance.new("IntValue")
    items.Name = "Items"
    items.Value = 0
    items.Parent = leaderstats

    local spaces = Instance.new("IntValue")
    spaces.Name = "Spaces"
    spaces.Value = 2
    spaces.Parent = leaderstats
end
```

Run the game to check that you can see these stats on the leaderboard.

While the game is running, take a look at the Explorer. If you open Players, you'll see that the leaderstats folder and variables have been attached to your character.

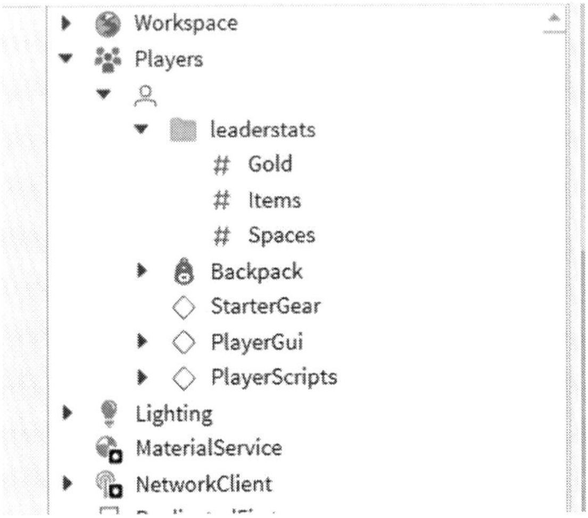

MAKING ITEMS TO HARVEST

Harvesting items is the first part of the game loop and will be one of the first things players do. Thus, they need something to harvest.

You can build something from scratch by using parts and then grouping them together as a model. Alternatively, use the Toolbox to find something instead. I chose @ropeccool's Pink Crystal. You can add this directly from the Toolbox or go to create.roblox.com and click on Marketplace. Search for the item you want and Click Get Model.

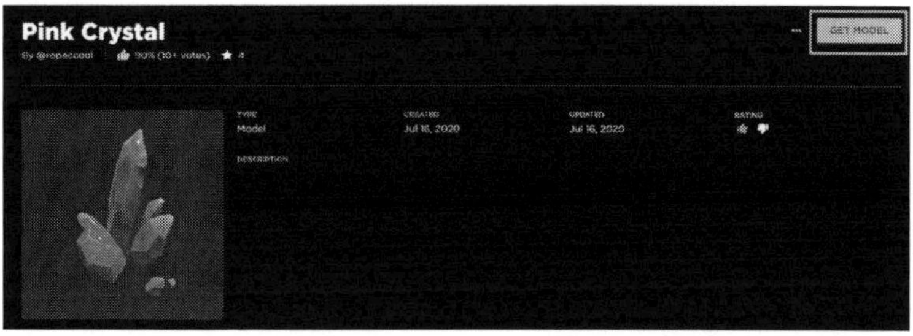

Items added through the Marketplace will be added to your Toolbox inventory.

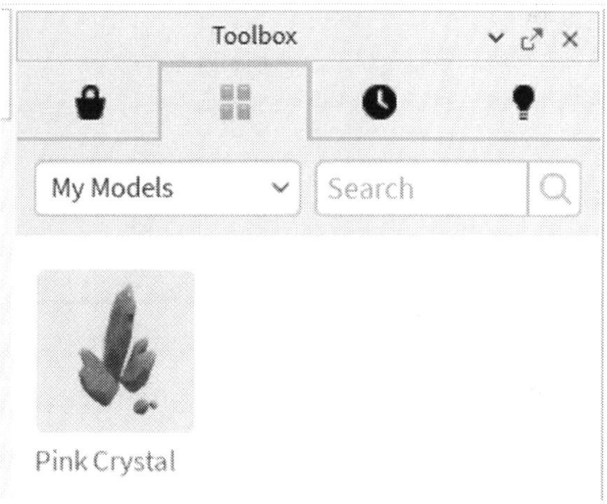

Add one to your experience and place it close to your spawn. Attach a BoolValue object and rename it canHarvest. Don't add multiple items just yet. It's easier to work with one until it's functional and then add more from there.

Select canHarvest and find its Value property. Make sure it's enabled. This is the equivalent of giving it the value true in code.

Creating a Tool

Now that we have an item to harvest, we need something to harvest it with. Go over to the Toolbox or Marketplace and look for a tool that matches your item. Look for models that have animations. I chose @gorosae's StarterTool. Insert it and drag it to the StarterPack. This will automatically include the tool into a player's backpack when they join the experience.

To test, run the game and see if you spawn in with a tool item.

CODING HARVEST MECHANICS

The logic is simple; to harvest an item, players need to touch it with the tool. Once the tool makes contact, the code should

- check whether the item is harvestable, and that the player has space.
- increase the Items stat.
- temporarily make the item disappear from the environment.

Tip: Most models have a Handle child or some other basepart to which a mesh is attached. For our code to work, your script needs to be attached to this part. We need a Touched event to harvest the item, but models don't have Collision properties and thus no Touched events. To remedy this, we need a basepart object like Handle through which to access Touched.

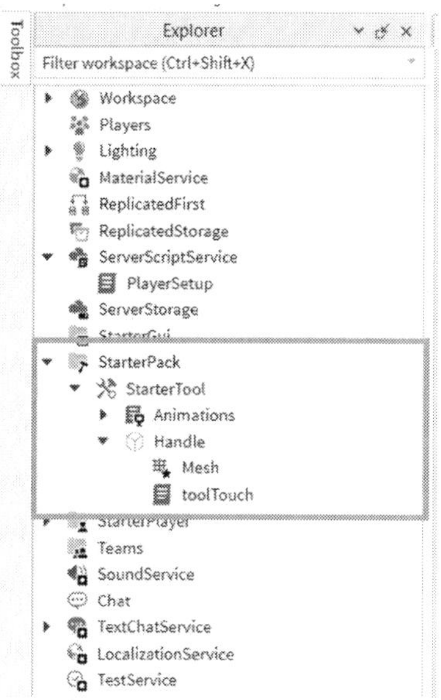

Try to code the mechanics I listed above on your own before looking at the example.

Touched Event

First, create a script and attach it to the Handle object. Then, create a variable to reference that handle as the tool. Code an onTouch function and connect it to the tool's Touched event.

```
local tool = script.Parent

local function onTouch(otherPart)

end

tool.Touched:Connect(onTouch)

```

To determine whether otherPart is a harvestable item, we test if it has a child called "canHarvest." In this case, we use FindFirstChild instead of FindFirstChildWhichIsA. The difference between these two functions lies in what they search for. The first searches for something with the name supplied as an argument. The latter searches by type. If we wanted to use FindFirstChildWhichIsA in this context, we would need to search for "BoolValue" instead of "canHarvest."

```
local tool = script.Parent

local function onTouch(otherPart)
    local canHarvest = otherPart:FindFirstChild("canHarvest")
    if canHarvest then
        print("part was touched")
    end
end

```

Run the game and try to harvest your item. Check that you see the print message.

Note: The if-statement will check whether canHarvest is present in otherPart; it does not test its value.

Next, we need to test whether the player has enough space for the item. Before we can do that, we need to access the player's stats. Create variables to reference the tool model, backpack (in which the tool is stored during gameplay), and finally the player themself.

```
local tool = script.Parent --the tool part handle
local toolitem = tool.Parent --the tool model
local backpack = toolitem.Parent --the backpack
local player = backpack.Parent --the player character

```

This might seem excessive, but it's necessary. The leaderstats folder is only created when a player joins the game, and to get to it, we need to first get to the player character.

Create three variables to reference the leaderstats folder and the items and spaces stats. Use FindFirstChild for all three.

```

local playerStats = player:FindFirstChild("leaderstats")
local items = playerStats:FindFirstChild("Items")
local spaces = playerStats:FindFirstChild("Spaces")

```

We want code that will check whether the player has enough space for a new item. One way of doing that is to check whether items' value is less than spaces' value with the condition items.Value < spaces.Value. We also need to check whether canHarvest is true by testing its .Value. Both these comparisons need to occur simultaneously in an if-statement.

In the if-statement, add code that will increase items by one.

```

local function onTouch(otherPart)
    local canHarvest = otherPart:FindFirstChild("canHarvest")
    if canHarvest then
        if canHarvest.Value == true and items.Value < spaces.Value then
            print("part was touched")
            items.Value = items.Value + 1
        end
    end
end

```

Run the game. Check to see that you can successfully touch the item and that your Items stat increases. If the code doesn't work, check that you reference all the names correctly and that you have .Value added for canHarvest, items, and spaces.

Making the Item Disappear

Once an item has been harvested, it should vanish temporarily. For this, its Transparency, CanCollide, and canHarvest should change to make it invisible and unharvestable. Add a wait time, and then reverse the changes to make it harvestable again.

```
local function onTouch(otherPart)
    local canHarvest = otherPart:FindFirstChild("canHarvest")
    if canHarvest then
        if canHarvest.Value == true and items.Value < spaces.Value then
            print("part was touched")
            items.Value = items.Value + 1

            --making the item disappear
            canHarvest.Value = false
            otherPart.Transparency = 1
            otherPart.CanCollide = false
            wait(5)

            --making it reappear
            canHarvest.Value = true
            otherPart.Transparency = 0
            otherPart.CanCollide = true
        end
    end
end

tool.Touched:Connect(onTouch)

--[[code adapted from
    https://create.roblox.com/docs/education/adventure-game-series/collect-items
    retrieved in April 2023]]
```

Run the game and test that the item disappears after being touched and then reappears after some time.

SELLING ITEMS

The second part of the game loop is selling the items that have been harvested. Create a space where your player can sell their items. Make something that fits your environment. For convenience, place it close to the SpawnLocation and item you created. I use a basic block with a SurfaceLight and TextLabel to act as a selling platform.

Attach a script to it and rename it accordingly. The platform should decrease Items to zero and increase Gold once the player steps on it. Go ahead and set up the Touched event and event handler and code a humanoid test and conditional.

```
local platform = script.Parent

local function onTouch(otherPart)
    local character = otherPart.Parent
    local humanoid = character:FindFirstChildWhichIsA("Humanoid")
    if humanoid then

    end
end

platform.Touched:Connect(onTouch)

```

Once again, to access the player stats, we need to get the player character. This time, we'll use game.Players:GetPlayerFromCharacter(humanoid.Parent). The Humanoid object is added into the player character found in Workspace. The leaderstats folder, on the other hand, is added to the character object in Players.

This function lets us access the Players object that corresponds to the one Humanoid is attached to.

```
local platform = script.Parent

local function onTouch(otherPart)
    local character = otherPart.Parent
    local humanoid = character:FindFirstChildWhichIsA("Humanoid")
    if humanoid then
        local player = game.Players:GetPlayerFromCharacter(humanoid.Parent)
    end
end

```

Add variables for the leaderstats folder, Items, and Gold, and include a print code to test the function.

```
local platform = script.Parent

local function onTouch(otherPart)
    local character = otherPart.Parent
    local humanoid = character:FindFirstChildWhichIsA("Humanoid")
    if humanoid then
        local player = game.Players:GetPlayerFromCharacter(humanoid.Parent)
        --get player stats
        local playerStats = player:FindFirstChild("leaderstats")
        local items = playerStats:FindFirstChild("Items")
        local gold = playerStats:FindFirstChild("Gold")
        print("player touched platform")
    end
end
```

Selling Mechanics

Create a second function that will process the sale. It should take gold and items as parameters.

Decide what your items should sell for. For example, one crystal is worth 100 gold. In your function, create a variable called totalSum. This variable will contain the number of items multiplied by the selling price.

```

local function sellItems(items, gold)
    local totalSum = items.Value * 100
end
```

To check that the math works, add a print to display the value of totalSum. Next, add this sum to the player's gold and decrease the value of items to zero. Once that's done, call the sellItems function from the onTouch.

```
local platform = script.Parent

local function sellItems(items, gold)
    local totalSum = items.Value * 100
    print(totalSum)
    gold.Value = gold.Value + totalSum
    items.Value = 0
end

local function onTouch(otherPart)
    local character = otherPart.Parent
    local humanoid = character:FindFirstChildWhichIsA("Humanoid")
    if humanoid then
        local player = game.Players:GetPlayerFromCharacter(humanoid.Parent)
        --get player stats
        local playerStats = player:FindFirstChild("leaderstats")
        local items = playerStats:FindFirstChild("Items")
        local gold = playerStats:FindFirstChild("Gold")
        print("player touched platform")
        sellItems(items, gold)
    end
end

platform.Touched:Connect(onTouch)

--[[code sourced from
    https://create.roblox.com/docs/education/adventure-game-series/selling-items
    retrieved in April 2023]]
```

Run the game. Check that once you touch the platform, the items and gold stats change correctly.

BUYING UPGRADES

Use the same steps to create an option to upgrade the number of spaces a player has. First, create the part through which the player will access an upgrade. In this case, I use a block with a display label. Then, add a clickDetector. With it, we'll use a different event;

instead of using part.Touched, we can use clickDetector.MouseClick. This event works the exact same way as Touched, except that we don't need to test for humanoid with it.

I want you to code this section on your own. The process is the same as above, with some minor changes. Once the player clicks the upgrade, their gold will decrease, and their spaces will increase. Try on your own before looking at the answer.

```
local button = script.Parent
local clickDeterctor = button.ClickDetector
local newSpaces = 5
local upgradeCost = 100

local function onClick (player)
    print("someone clicked the button")

    --get player stats
    local playerStats = player:FindFirstChild("leaderstats")
    local gold = playerStats:FindFirstChild("Gold")
    local spaces = playerStats:FindFirstChild("Spaces")

    if gold.Value >= upgradeCost then
        gold.Value = gold.Value - upgradeCost
        spaces.Value = newSpaces
    end
end

clickDeterctor.MouseClick:Connect(onClick)

--[[code sourced from
    https://create.roblox.com/docs/education/adventure-game-series/buying-upgrades
    retrieved in April 2023]]
```

FINAL TOUCHES

Once the game mechanics are up and running, you can add some final touches. When coding, we used relatively small values for things like wait times, upgrade costs, and inventory space. This made it easier to test the game but isn't suitable for actual gameplay. Go through the code and adjust these values to something more appropriate. Keep testing the game as you adjust these values to make sure they still work and that changes don't affect functionality.

Move the sell and upgrade objects to their proper positions and begin adding more harvestables. Duplicate the item you already have and move them into position. Then, take the time to flesh out your terrain more and turn it into a world players want to explore. Make sure that your items are accessible to players and that they won't struggle too much to reach them.

While you do this, consider what would be enjoyable for a player. Remember to test the game periodically. It's difficult to judge scale and distance when designing the environment, and sometimes you just need to play it and see things for yourself. Once you think the game is ready, ask someone else to play it as a final test before publishing it if you want to.

10

CREATE A BATTLE ROYALE

A battle royale is a multiplayer game where different players face off against each other to see who remains as the last one standing. They're typically fighting games but can also be any game where the goal is to eliminate other players.

PROJECT PLANNING

Before we start the project, we need to plan it out. This game has a lot of features and is more complex than the adventure game from the previous chapter. In it, we'll

- manage players.
- set up timers and events.
- create a user interface.

- define the start and end of matches.
- handle the aftermath of each round.

For it, you'll need to create two areas: one for the lobby and one for the arena. Take the time to sketch out a plan for both.

The lobby is going to be pretty simple. All you need is a walled-off space with a spawn location and whatever decorations you want to add.

For the arena, your plan should include multiple spawn points, obstacles, and walls to create enclosed spaces, and varying levels of playable space. Use basic shapes to get an idea of the layout you want. Think about where and how your players would move during a match. If you're stuck, try to imagine a fun place to hold a fight and then go from there.

The way this game will work is that players spawn into the lobby when they first join. Once there are enough players, they will be transported to an arena and a timer will start. Once a player dies, they will be transported to the lobby. The match will end when only one player remains, or the time runs out. Finally, the game resets and runs cleanup, which usually involves transporting any remaining players to the lobby, finding winners, and resetting the arena for the next match. A GUI will keep players informed of the time on the clock, the number of players remaining, and the status of the game.

CREATE THE MAP

Once you have planning sketches ready, create a new Baseplate project in Roblox Studio. Our two areas will essentially be two separate, floating rooms. We don't need a baseplate, so go ahead and remove it from the Workspace if you want to. Of course, you can also leave it in while building and then remove it later if you want to.

For the lobby, use base parts to create a walled-off space with a floor. Tip: To make the process easier, go to the Model tab and find the Snap to Grid sections. There, you'll be able to specify how the parts move when you transform them. Objects move according to studs, and you can change exactly how many studs they should move along. You can also change the angle of rotation here for more precise orientations.

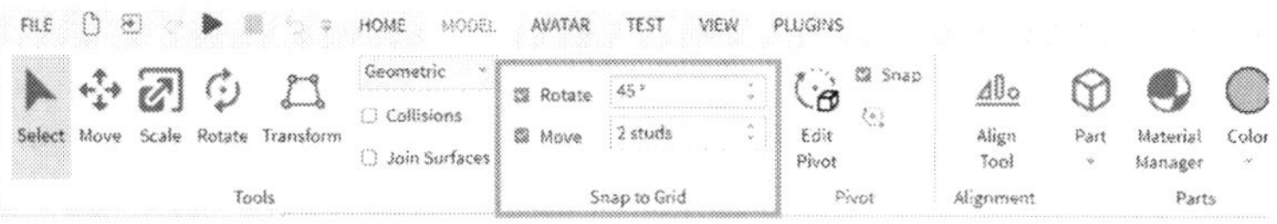

You can also go to View and enable the Show Grid option. These will help you align your objects more easily to each other.

When you add parts, group them together using models and folders. At the end of the day, all parts that are used in the lobby should be in a separate folder from the rest of the Workspace.

Here is my lobby:

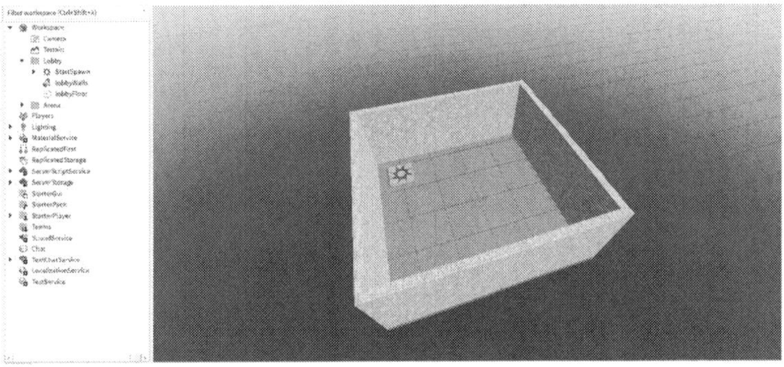

Building the arena won't be as simple. Create a new folder in your workspace. As you did for the lobby, create a room that will contain the match. We're going to use a technique called grayboxing where we use simple shapes to create the basic structure of the room you envisioned. Go to the Toolbox and click on the filter options.

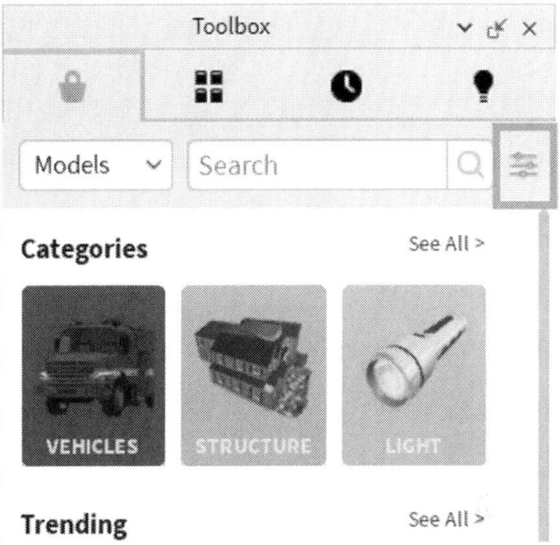

There, you'll be able to search for specific creators. Type in "Roblox_Educators" and select this one:

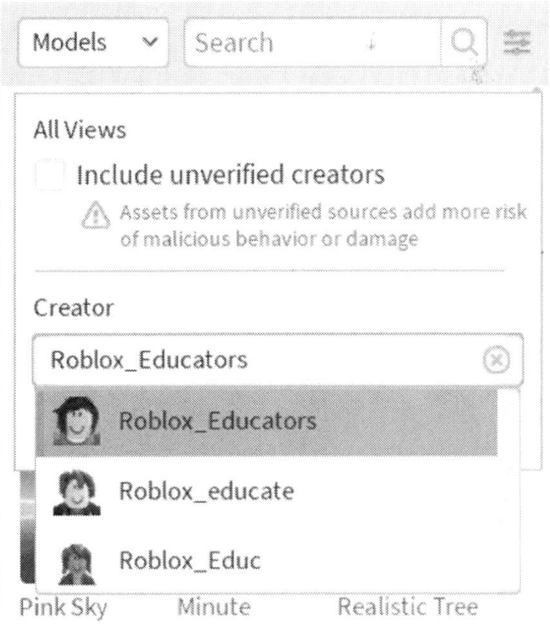

Hit apply. If you don't see their models show up, redo the search but select the "Include unverified creators" option. Roblox_Educators has a basic graybox assets kit that's freely available for your use.

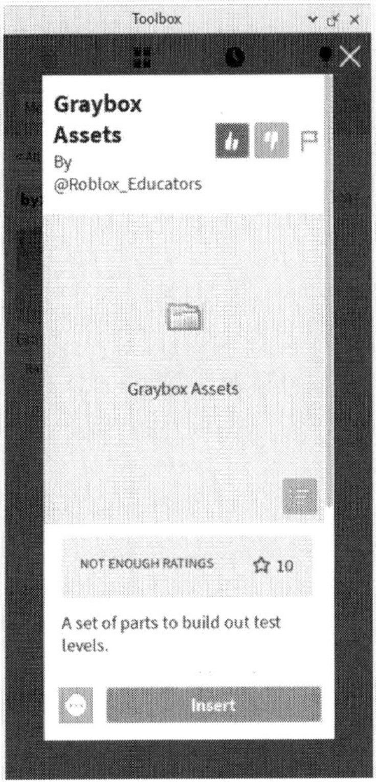

Click Insert and the entire kit will be added into your workspace. Use the shapes as you want and delete the ones you don't want to use. If you want multiple copies of one, simply duplicate it. Remember to move the assets into your arena folder. You can also use regular base parts if you want to.

Take the time to flesh out your arena. Use different shapes, sizes, and heights to add variety to the space. Include things like ramps, stairs, ladders, and various platforms to create a dimensional environment. Find places for multiple spawn locations. Matches will consist of multiple players, so consider how many participants you want in each round. If you want eight players, add eight spawn locations.

Try to keep your Workspace organized. Keep the spawn locations in one folder, related parts in another, and so on. If you have multiple parts that make up a single unit, group them together as a model. This will also help you scale and position them more accurately.

It's difficult to judge scale without playing in the environment, so make sure to regularly run the game and test the features you're adding. Make sure you can get around objects, reach the ones you want to jump on, and fit onto ramps. Once you're satisfied with the layout of the arena, run it a final time, and run through it like you would if you were a player in a match.

Don't start adjusting the look of the arena beyond this yet. Focus only on creating the layout of it. It's easier to make sure you have a working game before you spend time making it look nice.

CODING THE GAME LOOP

To begin, create a folder in ServerStorage called "ModuleScripts." In this folder, create two ModuleScripts, called GameSettings and MatchManager. GameSettings will store common values and variables that determine certain functional features. MatchManager will store functions and events related to the arena matches.

Next, go to ServerScriptService and create an ordinary script called GameManager. This script will call and manage code from other scripts. Since ModuleScripts cannot run code themselves, we need a regular script that will be able to call the code from these modules at the right times.

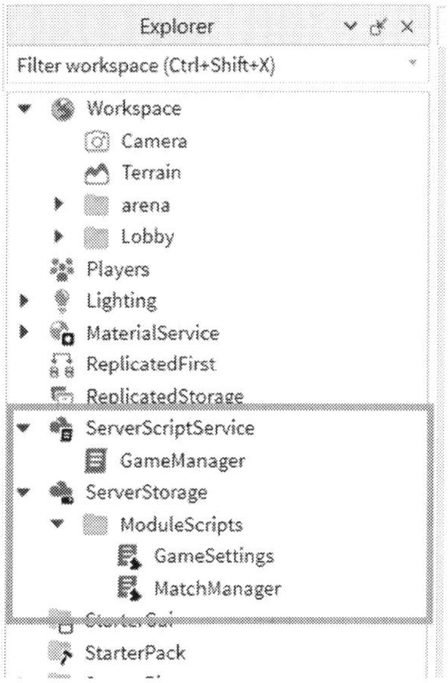

GameSettings

Let's quickly recap ModuleScripts. These scripts store different variables and functions as members of a module. This allows us to keep related code separate from other nonrelated code and helps us keep scripts better organized. The variables and functions contained in ModuleScripts exist as members of that module. To access them from other scripts, we import the module using "require()" and then access its members using moduleName.memberName.

In GameSettings, you'll find the autofilled module declaration and return module. Replace "module" with gameSettings. Do so for both the declaration and the return code at the bottom.

Next, create the following variables:

- intermissionTime: how long players will wait between matches
- matchDuration: how long each round or match will last
- minimumPlayers: the lowest number of players necessary for a match
- transitionTime: a brief pause between the changes from intermission to match and vice versa

For now, assign small values to each to make testing easier.

```
local gameSettings = {}

-- game variables added to the module
gameSettings.intermissionDuration = 5
gameSettings.matchDuration = 10
gameSettings.minimumPlayers = 2
gameSettings.transitionTime = 5

return gameSettings

--[[code sourced from https://create.roblox.com/docs/education/battle-royale-series/coding-the-game-loop#gamesettings-script
    retrieved in April 2023]]
```

MatchManager

This script will contain various functions related to the arena rounds. Replace "module" with matchManager. We aren't going to add too much to this script just yet. For now, create a module function called prepareGame and code a basic print statement in it.

```
local matchManager = {}

function matchManager.prepareGame()
    print("Game starting!")
end

return matchManager

--[[code sourced from https://create.roblox.com/docs/education/battle-royale-series/coding-the-game-loop#gamesettings-script
    retrieved in April 2023]]

```

When working in module scripts, there are two kinds of functions: namely, local functions and module functions. Local functions are declared with local scope and a name as usual. Module functions, on the other hand, are direct members of the module itself. It is not declared with local scope, and its name always includes the module name. For example, function matchManager.prepareGame().

GameManager

For this script to access the modules, create variables to store references to the ServerStorage, ModuleScripts folder, and the ModuleScripts. You'll also need a variable to reference the Players service. When importing a ModuleScript, we use the function require().

```
local ServerStorage = game:GetService("ServerStorage")
local Players = game:GetService("Players")

local moduleScripts = ServerStorage:WaitForChild("ModuleScripts")
local matchManager = require(moduleScripts:WaitForChild("MatchManager"))
local gameSettings = require(moduleScripts:WaitForChild("GameSettings"))
```

In the above example, I use the method WaitForChild. When we run the game, it's first run through the compiler and then built. This can sometimes take a few moments and means that objects like parts and scripts don't come online at the same time. If the code executes before they are built, it will try to find an object that doesn't exist, and an error will occur. WaitForChild tells the code to wait until the object comes into existence before moving on. If, for example, the GameManager code runs before the ModuleScripts folder is accessible, the game will wait for the folder and then store it as a reference. We'll use this method in most of the variable references moving forward. The only times we don't use it are when referencing services like Players or ServerStorage.

Since this game runs on a repetitive cycle of matches and intermissions, most of its code will need to be placed inside a while loop. Insert a basic while true do loop into this script.

```
local ServerStorage = game:GetService("ServerStorage")
local Players = game:GetService("Players")

local moduleScripts = ServerStorage:WaitForChild("ModuleScripts")
local matchManager = require(moduleScripts:WaitForChild("MatchManager"))
local gameSettings = require(moduleScripts:WaitForChild("GameSettings"))

while true do

end
```

CODING THE INTERMISSION

Starting Intermission

The intermission starts at the beginning of the game while it waits for enough players to run a match. For this, we need two main variables: the number of players in the experience (as stored under players in GameManager) and minimumPlayers (as per GameSettings).

Our code will compare the value of players to the value of minimumPlayers in GameManager to test if there are enough players. Once the player count is equal to or greater than minimumPlayers, the game can move from an intermission state to a match state. Currently, my minimumPlayers is set to 2, meaning there need to be at least two players in the lobby for the intermission to end.

How would you code this? Take a moment to consider the problem and try to think of a solution. If your answer is to use an if-statement to check a condition, you're halfway right. We do need to test a condition, but we can't do this with a simple conditional. Since we don't know when the minimum number of players will be reached, we cannot define when the condition needs to run. For this reason, we need code that will run multiple times to test it. The answer is to use a loop that tests a condition.

You have two options, a while loop, or a repeat loop. Both of them will test the condition for each iteration of the code. Since we've covered while loops, I'm going to use a repeat loop in this example. Know, however, that you can use a while loop to get exactly the same effect.

Repeat loops work on the same logic as while loops. They repeat code based on a condition. While loops use the structure "while condition do [code]." Repeat loops approach it from the other direction, and they use the structure "repeat [code] until condition." They essentially execute code repeatedly until the condition becomes true.

Try to construct a condition that will work for our purpose. Do this on your own first before reading further.

In the case of a while loop, we want code to loop while the number of players is less than minimumPlayers, thus players < minimumPlayers. In the case of a repeat loop, we want code to keep repeating until the number of players is equal to or greater than minimumPlayers, thus players >= minimumPlayers.

With all that in mind, construct the intermission loop in GameManager; it needs to go into the while loop that's already there. Inside the loop, code a basic print statement for testing purposes, and add a wait with the intermissionDuration value.

```
while true do
    repeat --intermission loop
        print("Starting intermission")
        wait(gameSettings.intermissionDuration)
    until Players.NumPlayers >= gameSettings.minimumPlayers
end
```

Run the game and check that you see the "Starting intermission" display in the output. Check that the message repeats within the time you defined in intermissionDuration.

Ending Intermission

Once there are enough players, the game should end the intermission and start the match. After the intermission loop, add a print statement to display "Intermission over" and add a wait code with the transitionTime variable as parameter. Then, call the prepareGame function from MatchManager.

```
while true do
    repeat --intermission loop
        print("Starting intermission")
        wait(gameSettings.intermissionDuration)
    until Players.NumPlayers >= gameSettings.minimumPlayers

    --moving out of intermission
    print("Intermission over")
    wait(gameSettings.transitionTime)
    matchManager.prepareGame()
end
```

To test this code, we need multiple players. As is, there need to be at least two players in the game for it to end the intermission. Regular testing won't cover this since you're only one character. For this, we need a local server to simulate multiple players. Go to the Test tab and find the Clients and Servers section. This gives you the option of hosting a test server with multiple characters. Select the option that matches your minimumPlayers value.

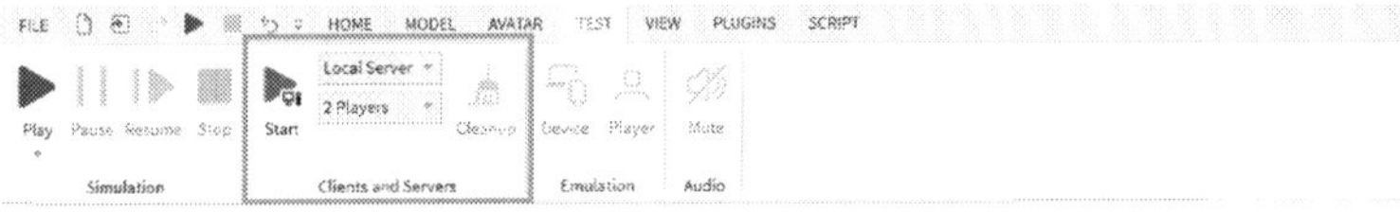

Once you hit start, Studio will open several new windows, a server, and then a client for each player in the experience. This can take some time, especially the first time you do it. It might also prompt you to give it security access. Click Allow Access if prompted and wait for all the windows to load in. Find the one marked as the Server; you'll be able to see the print statements in its Output. Check that you see the "Starting intermission" and "Intermission over"

messages. They'll keep repeating since we haven't provided any other code yet. Once you're satisfied, click the Cleanup button to close all the server-related windows.

If the game doesn't work as expected, make sure that you have all the names referenced correctly. If your objects are named differently than mine, your code will use different names. Use your Explorer to double-check the identifiers. Identify the statement that isn't printing and use it to pinpoint where the problem is. Check that the code there is in the right blocks. Finally, if the intermission isn't ending, check that the number of players you added to the local server is equal to or greater than minimumPlayers. If your minimum is four, you'll need four players.

MANAGING PLAYERS

All players are automatically spawned into the lobby at the start of the game. Once the match begins, they will be transported to the arena. Players will be returned to the lobby once they are defeated or if the match ends. For this, we need a way to manage different players.

Create a new ModuleScripts in the ServerStorage folder. Rename it PlayerManager and replace the "module" with playerManager. In the script, create variables to reference Players and ServerStorage.

```
local playerManager = {}
	--service variables
	local Players = game:GetService("Players")
	local ServerStorage = game:GetService("ServerStorage")

return playerManager

```

Next, create three variables called lobbySpawn, arenaSpawns, and the arena folder. These will store location references we need to transport players. Finally, create an empty table that will track active players.

```
local playerManager = {}

--service variables
local Players = game:GetService("Players")
local ServerStorage = game:GetService("ServerStorage")

--map variables
local lobbySpawn = workspace.Lobby.StartSpawn
local arenaMap = workspace.Arena
local spawnLocations = arenaMap.SpawnLocations

--player table
local activePlayers = {}

return playerManager

```

Make sure that you name them correctly. If your parts and folders are stored under different names, your code will need to reflect that. You don't need to reference each individual arena spawn location, just the folder in which they're kept. Make sure there's nothing else in that folder besides SpawnLocations.

Next, create a module function called sendPlayersToMatch. For now, it has no parameters and no code other than a print display.

```
--module functions
function playerManager.sendPlayersToMatch ()
    print("sending players to match")
end

```

Then, create a local function called onPlayerAdded with player as a parameter. We'll use this function to ensure that players spawn into the lobby and not one of the other spawns. As is, a player can spawn into any of the possible locations, and we want to make it so they can only spawn into the lobby. Where someone spawns are determined by their RespawnLocation property. This is attached to the player themself, and to access it, we need access to that player.

Using PlayerAdded will let us create a reference for each player as they're added. We can also set their RespawnLocation at the same time. In the function, write the code "player.RespawnLocation = lobbySpawn." Then, connect the function to the PlayerAdded event.

```
--local functions
local function onPlayerAdded (player)
    player.RespawnLocation = lobbySpawn
end

Players.PlayerAdded:Connect(onPlayerAdded)

return playerManager

--[[code sourced from https://create.roblox.com/docs/education/battle-royale-series/
managing-players
    retrieved in April 2023]]
```

To use these functions, we need to link them to the MatchManager module. Go to Matchmanager and create variables for ServerStorage, the ModuleScripts folder, and the PlayerManager script. Call the send-PlayersToMatch function from prepareGame.

```
local matchManager = {}

--PlayerManager variables
local serverStorage = game:GetService("ServerStorage")
local moduleScripts = serverStorage:WaitForChild("ModuleScripts")
local playerManager = require(moduleScripts:WaitForChild("PlayerManager"))

function matchManager.prepareGame()
    print("game is starting!")
    playerManager.sendPlayersToMatch()
end

return matchManager

--[[code sourced from https://create.roblox.com/docs/education/battle-royale-series/
managing-players
    retrieved in April 2023]]
```

Run the game with a local server. Make sure that all player characters join into the lobby and that you see the print message from sendPlayersToMatch. If you don't, go back and double-check that you used the right name for the lobbySpawn object when assigning the variable. You can also check other names and references for mistakes. Finally, double-check that you connected the onPlayerAdded function with the PlayerAdded event.

Transporting Players to the Arena

In PlayerManager, create a new local function called preparePlayer. It will take two parameters—player and whichSpawn. In its code block, set the player's

RespawnLocation to whichSpawn. This variable (whichSpawn) will contain a reference to one of the arena spawnLocations.

Then, use the built-in function LoadCharacter() to reload the player's position and transport them to the new spawn point. LoadCharacter essentially resets the player object with each reload. This is important for later features of the game.

```
local function preparePlayer (player, whichSpawn)
    player.RespawnLocation = whichSpawn
    player:LoadCharacter()
end

return playerManager
```

To determine where players load in, we have to identify each of the various arena spawns that are available. Create a variable called arenaSpawns and initialize it with spawnLocations:GetChildren(). This will essentially create an array of possible values that we can assign to whichSpawn.

Remember that empty table we created earlier called activePlayers? We're going to add players to it as they join the experience. This will help us track the players as well as assign their respawn locations.

First, create a for loop in the sendPlayersToMatch function. This loop will run through players:GetPlayers using pairs as though it were a dictionary. It uses playerKey for the key value, and whichPlayer to contain the name of the player. For each iteration, it will store the name of the player as a new entry of activePlayers.

```
--module functions
function playerManager.sendPlayersToMatch ()
    print("sending players to match")
    local arenaSpawns = spawnLocations:GetChildren()
    for playerKey, whichPlayer in pairs(Players:GetPlayers()) do
        table.insert(activePlayers,whichPlayer)
    end
end
```

In this same loop, create a local variable called spawnLocation that will take the value of the first entry of our arenaSpawns array (local spawnLocation = arenaSpawns[1]). Then, call preparePlayers, and pass whichPlayer and spawnLocation as arguments.

If you're confused, slow down a moment to think about it. This game's code can and will get complex, so take your time to work through the logic step by step. The variable whichPlayer contains the name of a specific player while spawnLocation contains a reference to a specific spawn. When their values are passed to preparePlayer, it will transport the player in question to the SpawnLocation identified by the variables. Then, the code will move on to the next player and spawnLocation.

```
--module functions
function playerManager.sendPlayersToMatch ()
    print("sending players to match")
    local arenaSpawns = spawnLocations:GetChildren()
    for playerKey, whichPlayer in pairs(Players:GetPlayers()) do
        table.insert(activePlayers,whichPlayer)
        local spawnLocation = arenaSpawns[1]
        preparePlayer(whichPlayer, spawnLocation)
        table.remove(arenaSpawns, 1)
    end
end
```

Run the game to test that your character respawns to the arena. Tip: If you don't want to boot up a local server each time to test these features, change your minimumPlayers in GameSettings to one. This will let you test the game normally. However, keep in mind that this game is intended for multiple players. While this code works for single and multiple players, make sure to increase the minimum every once in a while and test it with more than one player.

ADDING A TOOL

Find a weapon model that you would like your players to use. It can be any weapon or tool that fits the concept of the game you have in mind. I'm using @Roblox_Educators' *Battle Royale Weapon*.

In the previous chapter, we added the tool directly to the StarterPack so that players would have the tool immediately after joining. For this game, however, we won't be doing that. LoadCharacter resets a character regardless of what they had in their inventory, and it would still spawn them with the weapon if it was in the

StarterPack. However, it would be a neat feature if players don't have a tool while they're in the lobby but then get one when they enter the arena, don't you think?

For this, add the tool model to ServerStorage. Make sure it's not in the ModuleScripts folder. Then, return to PlayerManager and create a variable to reference that model. If you added it into its own folder, you'll need to include a variable for the folder as well.

```
--service variables
local Players = game:GetService("Players")
local ServerStorage = game:GetService("ServerStorage")
--map variables
local lobbySpawn = workspace.Lobby.StartSpawn
local arenaMap = workspace.Arena
local spawnLocations = arenaMap.spawns

--player variable
local activePlayers = {}
local playerWeapon = ServerStorage.Weapon
```

Turn to the preparePlayer function and add two variables there to represent the character and sword. While the above playerWeapon variable represents the model itself, the sword variable will represent a copy of that object that is attached to a specific player.

For character, initialize it using "player.Character or player.Character:Wait()." Using or in this case lets us add an alternative option for the game to ensure that it runs well. Like with WaitForChild, using Character:Wait gives the game the option to wait for the object to become available before trying to reference it. This will stop the game from throwing errors if it cannot immediately find a character object.

For sword, we will use the function Clone. This is a built-in function that lets us duplicate the playerWeapon model and attach it to the player character once the game moves into a match state.

```
local function preparePlayer (player, whichSpawn)
    player.RespawnLocation = whichSpawn
    player:LoadCharacter()

    local character = player.Character or player.CharacterAdded:Wait()
    local sword = playerWeapon:Clone()
    sword.Parent = character
end
```

Run the game and test that you receive a tool once you spawn into the arena. Check also that this tool isn't available to you while in the lobby during the intermission.

MATCH EVENTS

The code we have created thus far provides for starting and ending the intermission and teleporting players. Once they have been transported, however, the intermission will start again. To enable players to actually play a match, we need events to trigger the start of a new round (to pause the game loop) and signal the end of the match (to resume the game loop).

In ServerStorage, create a new folder called Events, and then attach two BindableEvent objects to it. Rename them matchStart and matchEnd, respectively.

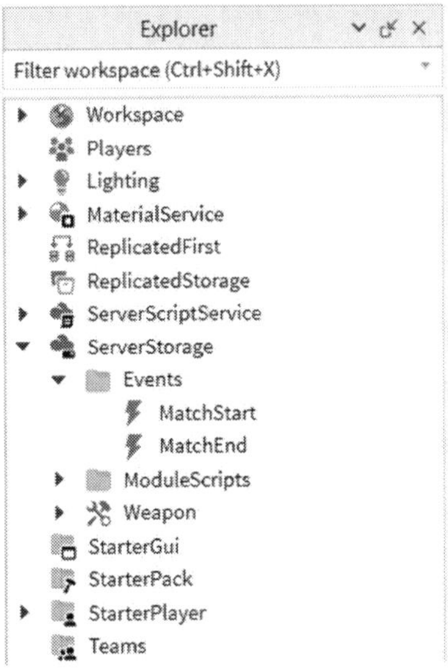

In GameManager, create two new variables to reference the Events folder and matchEnd event.

```
--event variables
local events = ServerStorage.Events
local matchEnd = events.MatchEnd
```

If you'll remember, when we want to access built-in functions of the BindableEvents class, we need to use .Event. One of these functions, called Wait, will let the script pause until matchEnd is triggered. In other words, we can use matchEnd.Event:Wait() to pause the game loop and stop the intermission from restarting until the match is over.

```
        --moving out of intermission
        print("Intermission over")
        wait(gameSettings.transitionTime)
        matchManager.prepareGame()

        --matchEnd
        matchEnd.Event:Wait()
end
```

TIMER

To set up a customizable timer, we are going to use a prebuilt timer module. Go to create.roblox.com and search for their Battle Royale tutorial. Under the Timers and Events section, there will be a subsection called "Setting Up The Timer." Here you will find a comprehensive timer module that you can copy and paste into your project. Look for this:

```
local Timer = {}
Timer.__index = Timer

function Timer.new()
    local self = setmetatable({}, Timer)

    self._finishedEvent = Instance.new("BindableEvent")
    self.finished = self._finishedEvent.Event

    self._running = false
    self._startTime = nil
    self._duration = nil
```

Once you have the code, create a new ModuleScript called Timer and paste the code you copied into it.

Then, require this module and GameSettings into MatchManager. From MatchManager, create a new instance of the timer module.

```
local gameSettings = require(moduleScripts:WaitForChild("GameSettings"))
local timer = require(moduleScripts:WaitForChild("Timer"))

local myTimer = timer.new()

```

This timer has access to all the functions set out in the module it was created from. This includes functions like start and stop that we can use to trigger matchStart and matchEnd.

Create two new functions in MatchManager called timeUp and startTimer. Add an appropriate print message to each. In startTimer, call the timer's start function and use gameSettings and matchDuration as the parameters. Then connect its .finished to our timeUp function.

```
local gameSettings = require(moduleScripts:WaitForChild("GameSettings"))
local timer = require(moduleScripts:WaitForChild("Timer"))

local myTimer = timer.new()

local function timeUp()
    print("time's up!")
end

local function startTimer()
    print("timer started")
    myTimer:start(gameSettings.matchDuration)
    myTimer.finished:Connect(timeUp)
end

```

Starting the Timer

In MatchManager, create three new variables for the events folder, matchStart, and matchEnd.

```
local playerManager = require(moduleScripts:WaitForChild("PlayerManager"))
local gameSettings = require(moduleScripts:WaitForChild("GameSettings"))
local timer = require(moduleScripts:WaitForChild("Timer"))

--event variables
local events = serverStorage:WaitForChild("Events")
local matchStart = events:WaitForChild("MatchStart")
local matchEnd = events:WaitForChild("MatchEnd")

local myTimer = timer.new()
```

Then, just above return, connect matchStart to start-Timer. Finally, fire startMatch from the prepareGame function.

```
function matchManager.prepareGame()
    print("game is starting!")
    playerManager.sendPlayersToMatch()
    matchStart:Fire()
end

matchStart.Event:Connect(startTimer)

return matchManager

--[[code sourced from https://create.roblox.com/docs/education/battle-royale-series/timers-and-events#setting-up-the-timer
    retrieved in April 2023]]
```

Run the game to make sure you can see the message that indicates the timer is starting.

CREATING A USER INTERFACE

Thus far, we've been using print and the Output window to communicate changes in the program.

However, players don't have access to the output and thus can't see the status of the game. So let's add an interface to display the status of the game to players.

GUI elements are generally added to the StarterGui to ensure that players can all see the same thing. The GUI communicates with clients, and each player is a unique client that needs to receive that information individually. As such, we need a way to guarantee consistent communication across all clients, and StarterGui does that.

In StarterGui, add a ScreenGui object and then a TextLabel. Rename the label ScreenDisplay.

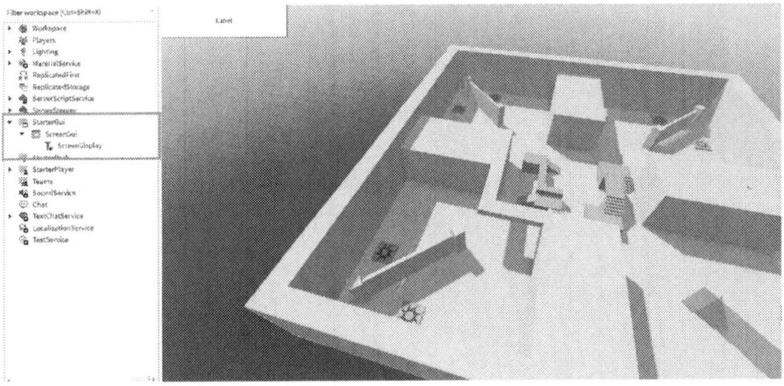

The label acts as a display board for players. If you want to change its location, click on it, and then drag it into position. You can also change its size.

Since GUIs communicate across the client-server boundary, the values it needs to access can't be in the ServerStorage. Go to ReplicatedStorage and create a new folder called Values. In it, add a StringValue and name it Status. Go to its properties and change its Value to "Welcome to the game!"

Then, attach a LocalScript to the TextLabel. Rename it DisplayStatus.

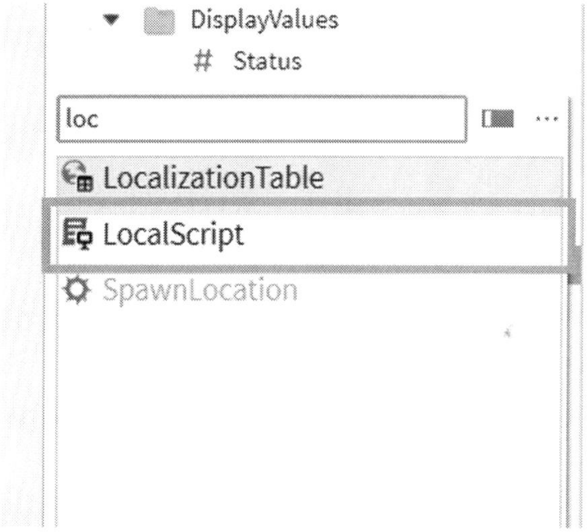

Open the script and create variables to reference ReplicatedStorage, the DisplayValues folder, and the Status string value. Finally, create a variable to store the text label the script is attached to.

The value currently in ReplicatedStorage contains the message we want to display. Its value will change depending on the status of the game. For example, while the game is in an intermission, Status will have a value of "waiting for players" or "in intermission." Once the game switches to a match, Status will also change.

To reflect this on the TextLabel, assign the TextLabel's Text property to the value contained in Status. Do this in a new function called updateText.

```
--display variables
local ReplicatedStorage = game:GetService("ReplicatedStorage")
local displayValues = ReplicatedStorage:WaitForChild("DisplayValues")
local status = displayValues:WaitForChild("Status")
local screenDisplay = script.Parent

local function updateText ()
    screenDisplay.Text = status.Value
end
```

Since Status's value will fluctuate with the game flow, we can use its Changed event to call the updateText function to change the GUI. Connect updateText to the Changed event and then, beneath it, call the updateText function. This will ensure more frequent updates.

```
--display variables
local ReplicatedStorage = game:GetService("ReplicatedStorage")
local displayValues = ReplicatedStorage:WaitForChild("DisplayValues")
local status = displayValues:WaitForChild("Status")
local screenDisplay = script.Parent

local function updateText ()
    screenDisplay.Text = status.Value
end

status.Changed:Connect(updateText)
updateText()

--[[code sourced from https://create.roblox.com/docs/education/battle-royale-series/creating-a-gui
    retrieved in April 2023]]
```

Run the game. Check that the display changes to the value you assigned to status. If it doesn't, make sure you use the TextLabel's .Text property and status's .Value.

DisplayManager

Take a moment to think about how the game works. We want a GUI that will inform the player of the various statuses the game goes through during its game loop. How would you go about making that happen?

To let the GUI change along with the rest of the game, we need to manage it the way we've managed everything else. Create a new ModuleScript called DisplayManager in the same folder as the other ModuleScripts. In it, create variables for ReplicatedStorage, displayStatus, and status.

```
local displayManager = {}

local ReplicatedStorage = game:GetService("ReplicatedStorage")
local displayValues = ReplicatedStorage:WaitForChild("DisplayValues")
local status = displayValues:WaitForChild("Status")

```

This module will contain code that manages the status updates. Then, call it from GameManager to run alongside the other modules. Next, create a module function called updateStatus. Here, code will manage the value of status. In the previous section, we made it so that the TextLabel displays status each time it changes, and in updateStatus, we can assign a new value to be displayed.

```
local displayManager = {}

local ReplicatedStorage = game:GetService("ReplicatedStorage")
local displayValues = ReplicatedStorage:WaitForChild("DisplayValues")
local status = displayValues:WaitForChild("Status")

--local functions

--module functions
function displayManager.updateStatus(newStatus)
    status.Value = newStatus
end

return displayManager

--[[code sourced from https://create.roblox.com/docs/education/battle-royale-series/creating-a-gui
    retrieved in April 2023]]
```

This function takes the parameter newStatus, which will contain the replacement value.

Updating Status

Now that we have that, let's go over to gameManager to code the change in status to feed to this function. Add variables for ReplicatedStorage and the displayManager module.

```
--services
local ServerStorage = game:GetService("ServerStorage")
local Players = game:GetService("Players")
local ReplicatedStorage = game:GetService("ReplicatedStorage")

--module scripts
local moduleScripts = ServerStorage:WaitForChild("ModuleScripts")
local matchManager = require(moduleScripts:WaitForChild("MatchManager"))
local gameSettings = require(moduleScripts:WaitForChild("GameSettings"))
local displayManager = require(moduleScripts:WaitForChild("DisplayManager"))

```

The very first thing the game should do is update the status to "Waiting for players" while the intermission is active. In the very first line after the while loop declaration, add the code to call the updateStatus function and pass it the message you want to display. You can remove the print statement from the repeat loop since the message will be displayed on the GUI.

```
while true do
    displayManager.updateStatus("Waiting for players")

    repeat --intermission loop
        wait(gameSettings.intermissionDuration)
    until Players.NumPlayers >= gameSettings.minimumPlayers

```

Next, replace the print "intermission is over" message with one that changes the status to "Match is starting." Again, this replaces the output display since the label itself acts as a means to test the code.

```
    --moving out of intermission
    displayManager.updateStatus("Match is starting")
    wait(gameSettings.transitionTime)
    matchManager.prepareGame()

    --matchEnd
    matchEnd.Event:Wait()
end
```

Run the game and check if the text label changes as the game does. If it doesn't, check that you're referencing the correct names when assigning variables and that you call updateStatus in the correct places.

Match Displays

Aside from displaying the current state of the game, we also want the GUI to display certain match statistics, like the amount of time left and the number of players still remaining. To do that, create two IntValue objects in DisplayValues; rename them playersLeft and TimeLeft. Create two variables to reference them in displayManager.

```
local displayManager = {}

local ReplicatedStorage = game:GetService("ReplicatedStorage")
local displayValues = ReplicatedStorage:WaitForChild("DisplayValues")
local status = displayValues:WaitForChild("Status")
local timeLeft = displayValues:WaitForChild("TimeLeft")
local playersLeft = displayValues:WaitForChild("PlayersLeft")

--local functions
```

Create a new module function called updateMatch-Status that will change the value of status to include playersLeft and timeLeft. Then, connect both values to a Changed event and the function.

```
--local functions
local function updateMatchStatus()
    status.Value = "Time left: "..timeLeft.Value.." / Players left: "..playersLeft.Value
end

--module functions
function displayManager.updateStatus(newStatus)
    status.Value = newStatus
end

timeLeft.Changed:Connect(updateMatchStatus)
playersLeft.Changed:Connect(updateMatchStatus)

return displayManager
```

The value you see assigned to status uses a technique called string building. This is when we combine different values into one string value, often for display purposes. It lets us craft values like timeLeft and player-sLeft into a meaningful message. We use the concate-nate operator here to mash different data types together. In this example, we combine strings with numbers. In print, we can use commas, but not when creating a value to assign to a variable.

The next step is to get the values that will be displayed in those variables. For playersLeft, turn to the PlayerManager script and create variables to store ReplicatedStorage, DisplayValues, and playersLeft.

```
--service variables
local Players = game:GetService("Players")
local ServerStorage = game:GetService("ServerStorage")
local ReplicatedStorage = game:GetService("ReplicatedStorage")

local lobbySpawn = workspace.Lobby.StartSpawn
local arenaMap = workspace.Arena
local spawnLocations = arenaMap.spawns
local displayValues = ReplicatedStorage:WaitForChild("DisplayValues")
local playersLeft = displayValues:WaitForChild("PlayersLeft")
```

The value of playersLeft should be the length of the activePlayers array. Its length represents the number of players that each match starts out with. This will later change as we begin coding when players are removed from the match.

```
--module functions
function playerManager.sendPlayersToMatch ()
    print("sending players to match")
    local arenaSpawns = spawnLocations:GetChildren()
    for playerKey, whichPlayer in pairs(Players:GetPlayers()) do
        table.insert(activePlayers,whichPlayer)
        local spawnLocation = arenaSpawns[1]
        preparePlayer(whichPlayer, spawnLocation)
        table.remove(arenaSpawns, 1)
    end
    playersLeft.Value = #activePlayers
end
```

Tip: Our code is becoming complex, and it's getting more and more difficult to manage the various variables, functions, and modules. We're also jumping around between scripts a lot. Now more than ever, use comments to create sections in your code and use white space to your advantage. This project is a good example of how proper organization can help make sense of code.

Find the startTimer function we created earlier. Underneath the finished event connection but before the function's end, create a while loop with the condition myTimer:isRunning(). Then, add the code "timeLeft.Value = (math.floor(myTimer:getTimeLeft() + 1))." Add "wait()" but do not pass a value into this wait. This will allow the game to manage its own time for better accuracy.

```
local function startTimer()
    print("timer started")
    myTimer:start(gameSettings.matchDuration)
    myTimer.finished:Connect(timeUp)

    while myTimer:isRunning() do
        timeLeft.Value = (math.floor(myTimer:getTimeLeft() + 1))
        wait()
    end
end
```

Lua has a math library with functions (like floor) that let us perform more complex math like conversions and trigonometry. The function math.floor rounds the number passed as argument to the nearest integer value (i.e., whole number). This particular line of code takes the value left in myTimer, adds 1 to it, and then rounds it out to the nearest whole number. For example, if there are 5.4 seconds left, it will increase it to 6.4, and then round it out to 6. This accounts for the milliseconds that pass between each second without overburdening the game by displaying each of those minuscule changes.

ENDING MATCHES

Respawn Defeated Players

Players are eliminated when their health is decreased to zero. The actual elimination is managed by the weapon's scripts. If you used a model from the Toolbox, it likely comes with a script that determines what happens when it hits another player. If it doesn't, find another tool that does, or refer to the trap exercise from Chapter 6 to create one that reduces the other player's health on contact. As extra practice, try to code a script for this on your own, even if your weapon already has one. I'll include a very basic example of what it would look like without any animations or special moves.

```
local players = game:GetService("Players")
local tool = script.Parent
local damage = 5

local function attack (opponent)
    local character = opponent.Parent
    local humanoid = character:FindFirstChildWhichIsA("Humanoid")
    if humanoid then
        humanoid.Health = humanoid.Health - damage
    end
end

local function onTouch (otherPlayer)
    attack(otherPlayer)
end

tool.Touched:Connect(onTouch)
```

As is, when a player is defeated, they'll be respawned into the arena when they should be removed from the match and be taken to the lobby instead.

In PlayerManager, create a new function called respawnToLobby. Make sure that it's somewhere before the preparePlayer function. Use it to set the player's new spawn point as the lobbySpawn, and then use the LoadCharacter function to reset them.

```

local function respawnToLobby(player)
    player.RespawnLocation = lobbySpawn
    player:LoadCharacter()
end

local function preparePlayer (player, whichSpawn)
```

Roblox has a built-in event that automatically references when a character dies. This event is named Died and is attached to the Humanoid object. We can use this event to determine when players should be removed from the arena and taken back to the lobby.

Find the preparePlayer function. At the end, declare a new variable to store a reference to humanoid. Use "character:WaitForChild("Humanoid")." Then, connect humanoid.Died to an anonymous function.

If you'll remember, anonymous functions are functions that aren't named. In this case, using an anonymous function will let us define it in the brackets of Died:Connect so that we can also reference who died specifically. Remember, we are using an array to track active players, and when one dies, we want to remove them from that array. This will also let us decrease the value of our playersLeft value in the GUI.

Code the connect event like you normally would. In this case, it's humanoid.Died:Connect(). In the brackets of Connect, type function () and then press enter to autofill the "end." Make sure it is still within the brackets of the Connect. You should see this:

```
local function preparePlayer (player, whichSpawn)
    player.RespawnLocation = whichSpawn
    player:LoadCharacter()

    local character = player.Character or player.CharacterAdded:Wait()
    local sword = playerWeapon:Clone()
    sword.Parent = character

    --respawn after death
    local humanoid = character:WaitForChild("Humanoid")

    humanoid.Died:Connect(function ()

    end)
end
```

In the anonymous function's block, call respawnTo-Lobby and pass player as a parameter to it.

```
    --respawn after death
    local humanoid = character:WaitForChild("Humanoid")

    humanoid.Died:Connect(function ()
        respawnToLobby(player)
    end)
end
```

END STATES

A match can end in two ways: when the time runs out or there's only one player left standing. Since they're two very different outcomes, we'll need to manage them separately.

Timer Ending

In GameSettings, create a new table called endStates. In it, declare two members called foundWinner and timerUp. Give them string values.

```
gameSettings.transitionTime = 5

gameSettings.endStates = {
    foundWinner = "foundWinner",
    timerUp = "timerUp"
}

return gameSettings
```

Once that's done, return to GameManager and find "matchEnd.Event:Wait()." Assign it to a variable by adding "local endState =" in front of it:

```
    --matchEnd
    local endState = matchEnd.Event:Wait()
    print("match ended with", endState)
end
```

For the sake of testing, add a print statement to display its value. It won't work just yet.

In MatchManager, find the timeUp function. Replace its print statement with code that will fire the matchEnd event and pass it gameSettings.endStates.-timerUp as a parameter.

```
local myTimer = timer.new()

local function timeUp()
    matchEnd:Fire(gameSettings.endStates.timerUp)
end

```

Run the game; test that you see timerUp displayed in the output once the time runs out.

Finding a Winner

In PlayerManager, declare variables for the ModuleScripts folder, GameSettings, the events folder, and matchEnd event.

```
--service variables
local Players = game:GetService("Players")
local ServerStorage = game:GetService("ServerStorage")
local ReplicatedStorage = game:GetService("ReplicatedStorage")

--module scripts
local moduleScripts = ServerStorage:WaitForChild("ModuleScripts")
local gameSettings = moduleScripts:WaitForChild("GameSettings")

--event variables
local events = ServerStorage:WaitForChild("Events")
local matchEnd = events:WaitForChild("MatchEnd")
```

Then, add a new function above respawnToLobby and call it checkPlayerCount. Add code to it that will check if the length of activePlayers is 1, and then add code to fire the matchEnd event. Reference the foundWinner object in its parameters.

```
local function checkPlayerCount()
    if #activePlayers == 1 then
        matchEnd:Fire(gameSettings.endStates.FoundWinner)
    end
end
```

This function will test how many players are left in activePlayers each time it is called. Once there is only one person left in the array, the function will end the match with the FoundWinner end state.

Removing Players from activePlayers

When a player dies, they are removed from the arena, but not from this array. To fix that, we need code that will remove defeated players. This will also let us use the array to identify the winner.

Create a function called removeActivePlayer (still in PlayerManager). It should be placed directly under checkPlayerCount in the script. Give it player as an argument.

```
local function removeActivePlayer(player)

end
```

It will loop through activePlayers to find a match for the player it receives as argument.

```lua
local function removeActivePlayer(player)
    for playerKey, whichPlayer in pairs(activePlayers) do
        if whichPlayer == player then

        end
    end
end
```

If it finds a match, that entry should be removed from activePlayers, and the value of playersLeft should be adjusted. Then, the checkPlayerCount function should be called to check how many entries are left in the array.

```lua
local function removeActivePlayer(player)
    for playerKey, whichPlayer in pairs(activePlayers) do
        if whichPlayer == player then
            table.remove(activePlayers, playerKey)
            playersLeft.Value = #activePlayers
            checkPlayerCount()
        end
    end
end
```

Scroll down until you find preparePlayer. Find the .Died connect code where we defined the anonymous function. In it, call removeActivePlayer the same way you called respawnToLobby.

```lua
    humanoid.Died:Connect(function ()
        respawnToLobby(player)
        removeActivePlayer(player)
    end)
end
```

Stopping the Timer

When a winner is found before the time runs out, the timer will keep going. To fix this, we need to stop the timer once a winner has been identified. To do this is pretty simple. Go to MatchManager and add a new function called stopTimer. I'd recommend putting it above timeUp, but anywhere above the event connection is fine. To stop the timer, use the code "myTimer:stop()."

```
local function stopTimer ()
    myTimer:stop()
end

```

Once you've done that, scroll to the bottom of the script where you connected matchStart to startTimer. There, connect matchEnd to stopTimer.

```
matchStart.Event:Connect(startTimer)
matchEnd.Event:Connect(stopTimer)

return matchManager
```

UPDATING THE GUI

Now that the code works, let's update the GUI to match. We'll need two more functions in PlayerManager. The first will be a module function called getWinnerName that will retrieve the winner's name.

```

function playerManager.getWinnerName ()

end

```

In it, write code to access the remaining player in activePlayers. I do this with an if-statement to avoid any errors if, for some reason, it tries to run with an empty array. Next, add code that creates a new variable, winningPlayer, that stores the value of activePlayers[1]. Then, return winningPlayer.Name.

```
function playerManager.getWinnerName ()
    if activePlayers[1] then
        local winningPlayer = activePlayers[1]
        return winningPlayer.Name
    end
end
```

Now we can use this in the second function called getEndStatus. This is a module function in MatchManager that takes endState as a parameter. In it, create an empty variable that will hold the result.

```

function matchManager.getEndStatus(endState)
    local statusToReturn
end

```

Use an if-elseif statement to test whether the game ended with foundWinner or timerUp by testing endState.

```
function matchManager.getEndStatus(endState)
    local statusToReturn

    if endState == gameSettings.endStates.foundWinner then

    elseif endState == gameSettings.endStates.timerUp then

    end

end
```

The variable statusToReturn will eventually store the value we want to display to the GUI. Its final value will depend on the outcome of these conditions. If a winner was found, we want to include the name of that player. We'll thus have to use the getWinnerName function, and then use its return as a string for display.

```
function matchManager.getEndStatus(endState)
    local statusToReturn

    if endState == gameSettings.endStates.foundWinner then
        local winnerName = playerManager.getWinnerName()
        statusToReturn = "Winner is : " .. winnerName

    elseif endState == gameSettings.endStates.timerUp then

end
```

If the time runs out, the value of statusToReturn will simply be something like "time ran out!" Finally, add an else condition, and then return statusToReturn outside the conditional. Make sure you have an end for both the if-statement and the function.

```
function matchManager.getEndStatus(endState)
    local statusToReturn

    if endState == gameSettings.endStates.foundWinner then
        local winnerName = playerManager.getWinnerName()
        statusToReturn = "Winner is : " .. winnerName
    elseif endState == gameSettings.endStates.timerUp then
        statusToReturn = "Time ran out!"
    else statusToReturn = "Error occurred"
    end

    return statusToReturn
end
```

To display this, go to GameManager and scroll down to the bottom. Find the print statement that displayed the value endState. Replace it with a new local variable called endStatus and call the getEndStatus function from it. The variable endStatus will thus reflect the value of statusToReturn. Then, use endStatus and the display function updateStatus to update the GUI.

Finally, add a wait time with timerDuration as a parameter.

```lua
        --matchEnd
        local endState = matchEnd.Event:Wait()
        local endStatus = matchManager.getEndStatus(endState)
        displayManager.updateStatus(endStatus)

        wait(gameSettings.transitionTime)

    end
```

CLEANUP

That does it for functional gameplay code. All that's left to do now is tidy up the remaining loose ends. As is, some players leave the arena with their weapons. To fix this, go to PlayerManager and create a new local function removePlayerWeapons with the parameter whichPlayer. In this function, create a conditional to test whether whichPlayer still exists (players have a tendency to quit the game when they die, which can cause an error). Store their Character part in a variable, and then use it to find the weapon object. If the weapon is there, the function should destroy it.

```lua
local function removePlayerWeapon(whichPlayer)
    if whichPlayer then
        local character = whichPlayer.Character

        if character:FindFirstChild("Weapon") then
            character.Weapon:Destroy()
        end
    end
end
```

Next, create a module function called removeAll-Weapons. This one will loop through activePlayers and remove the weapons of all players still in it.

```
function playerManager.removeAllWeapons()
    for playerKey, whichPlayer in pairs(activePlayers) do
        removePlayerWeapon(whichPlayer)
    end
end
```

Switch to MatchManager to create a separate CleanUp function. For now, this will only call removeAll-Weapons, but if you end up expanding the game and adding more features, you can use this function as a collection point for all other cleanup functions. Lastly, go to GameSettings, and call cleanUp before the final wait.

```
function matchManager.cleanUp()
    playerManager.removeAllWeapons()
end
```

The only thing left now is to transport remaining players to the lobby and clear the activePlayers array. Go to playerManager and create a module function resetMatch. In it, set up a loop to run through the activePlayers array. Whichever players are still left in the game will be in here. They need to go back to the lobby, so call respawnToLobby. After the loop's end, clear the array.

```lua
function playerManager.resetPlayers ()
    for playerKey, whichPlayer in ipairs(activePlayers) do
        respawnToLobby(whichPlayer)
    end
    activePlayers = {}
end

```

Go to MatchManager and create a resetMatch function that will call resetPlayers.

```lua
function matchManager.resetMatch()
    playerManager.resetPlayers()
end

```

Then, from GameSettings, call it after the final wait statement. I place it after the wait to give victors an extra moment in the arena before taking them to the lobby. If you don't want to do this, you can just call resetMatch from cleanUp to execute it at the same time as removeAllWeapons.

```lua
    matchManager.cleanUp()

    wait(gameSettings.transitionTime)

    matchManager.resetMatch()
end

--[[code sourced from https://create.roblox.com/docs/education/battle-royale-series/cleanup-and-reset
    retrieved in April 2023]]
```

FINAL TOUCHES

That was a pretty big project, and it isn't quite finished yet. The values we assigned in GameSettings were kept small for testing purposes. If you want to make this a proper game, those values need to be adjusted for proper gameplay. Remember to play your game periodically to test the values.

There's also the matter of making the project look like a game. As of yet, the maps are still very unfinished, but now that the game is working, you can take the time to make it look nice. Spend some time with this one, you've worked hard on it. Play around with visual styles and really flesh out the maps you have. Add decorations, textures, and extra features as you see fit. Once you're happy with it, you can publish it to Roblox if you want to.

11

CODING CHALLENGES

In this chapter, you'll find extra coding challenges. These are a bit harder than the projects we did previously, so take your time with them. I'm not going to give you answers to these challenges, but I will give you some insight into them. I want you to think about the problems and find your own solutions. A good developer knows how to solve problems and find answers to issues they haven't encountered before—so use this chapter to develop those skills.

These challenges were created by user starmaq on devforum.roblox.com, and they do a fantastic job of explaining their work and providing solutions. They also have a few extra challenges I didn't include if you want more. You can find these challenges and their answers at https://devforum.roblox.com/t/list-of-coding-challenges/485248.

#1 – NUMBERS TO FRENCH

French has a notoriously complex numerical system with several odd rules, which makes it the perfect language to test your problem-solving skills. Create an algorithm that will take a number and translate it into written French. If you don't know any French, take the time to look up its language rules for numbering. If French is too hard, use another language.

Method:

1. Identify unique values that are translated the same regardless of context and assign them to a table. In French, this means the numbers 0–16. Notice the correlation between value and index. For example, 0 is at [1], 1 at [2], and 2 at [3].
2. Assign multiples of 10 to a second table. Again, notice the relationship between value and index number. For example, 10 is at [1], 20 at [2], and 30 at [3].
3. Create a third table for the powers of 10, i.e., 10, 100, 1,000, etc.

4. Break numbers up into sections. For example, the number 1,359,876 can be broken up into millions (1), thousands (359), and tens and hundreds (876). Each of these chunks can then be further broken down. In 876, the first number (8) represents hundreds, the second (7) tens, and the third (6) is ones. With 359, the first (3) is hundred thousands, the second (5) is ten thousands, and the third (9) is thousands.
5. With that in mind, code the conversion. Make code that will test if the number can be translated directly from the tables. If not, the code should break the number up as we did above, convert it into a manageable format, and then start finding matches from the tables you created. Make sure to provide for any special translations (like the numbers 90–99 in French, which are translated differently from other numbers).
6. Combine your various functions together to craft a single string.

#2 – SORT A TABLE

Arrays, as you know, are ordered lists. The order of values is determined by the index number. But what if you wanted to change that order based on the values and not the indexes? Sorting algorithms are code that tests and compares the values of array elements and then changes their location based on specific criteria. Think of alphabetizing names, or sorting based on scores.

Try to create an algorithm of your own that will sort an array of numbers in descending order (i.e., from largest to smallest). Again, consider how you would do it. Break that process down into simple steps. For example, I would identify two specific entries, compare their values to see which one was larger, and then swap them based on the answer. Find a way to translate that into code.

Explore different methods of sorting. One method is quick sorting, where you define a pivot point to create a partition in the array. Then use two pointers to move through the different sides to find values that are lesser than or greater than the pivot. Once both pointers find values that match, they swap them. Another way is to use bubble sort to compare two adjacent elements, e.g., [1] and [2]. If [2] is greater than [1], swap them. Then compare [2] and [3] and repeat the process until the array is sorted; this can take several passes.

There's no right or wrong way to do this, so play around with a few different ideas.

#3 – NON-REPEATING CHARACTERS

For this challenge, create code that will run through a string to find and display the first character that isn't repeated anywhere else.

```
--strings

"aabgafdd" --b, g, and f are non-repeating

"rgggtffkrr" --t is non-repeating

"vvssfgfg" --no non-repeating characters
```

If there are no non-repeating characters, display an underscore.

The simplest solution is to sort through the string, identify each character, and test it against the others. If there are no matches, it is non-repeating. Alternatively, you can split the string wherever it finds a specified character and then test how many sections you end up with. If a string is split by a non-repeating character, there will be two sections while there would be more if the character repeats itself.

Here are three string manipulation functions that might help:

- match(string, pattern, initial): finds matches in a source string. String is the source, pattern the character you're looking for, and initial a numerical value that indicates where to start searching.
- split(string, separator): splits the string wherever it finds the separator value.
- sub(string, i, j): returns a substring from string position i to j.

#4 – FINDING THE FIRST DUPLICATE

Following the previous example, create an algorithm that will search through an array of numbers to find the first duplicate value. Use the same logic as above but apply it to a table with numbers. In this case, use loops to store a value and then compare it to other elements of the array. Return and display the value of the first duplicate you find.

#5 – ROTATING A MATRIX

Take a 2D table and rotate it 90 degrees clockwise.

```
--go from this
   {{1,2,3},
    {4,5,6},
    {7,8,9}}

--to this
   {{7,4,1},
    {8,5,2},
    {9,6,3}}
```

This challenge uses a 2D table or matrix (an array that contains other arrays). Data in these tables are organized into rows and columns. Each subarray forms a row and is stored under an index value. For example, the row {1,2,3} is stored at [1]. Corresponding indexes of different rows form a column. For example row1[1], row2[1], and row3[1] create the first column that reads {1,4,7}. Thus, {1,2,3} is the first row while {1,4,7} is the first column.

To rotate the table, you would need to adjust the values so that the first column becomes the top row, the top row becomes the third column, and so on.

#6 – PAIRS DIVISIBLE BY FIVE

For your next challenge, code an algorithm that will take two numbers (x and y) and find all possible pairs where m + n divided by 5 equals a whole number. M will be all numbers between 1 and x (1 <= m <= x), while n is all numbers between 1 and y (1 <= n <= y). In other words, x and y are the upper limits, and m and n include all numbers between 1 and them.

For example, if I give you the numbers 6 (x) and 12 (y), m will be 2–6, while n will be 2–12. In this example, there are 14 pairs that can work.

Tip: Use the operator "%" instead of "/" since it will test the residual and not the result. Finally, your code should return a number value to show how many pairs were successful. If you're still a little lost, consider this: A pair must satisfy the condition "(m+n)%5==0" to qualify as a divisible pair. Your function should take two integers and find how many pairs succeed that condition.

#7 – SNAKE_CASE TO CAMELCASE

This challenge is a bit easier. Write code that will convert a string from snake_case to camelCase. As you can guess, snake_case separates lowercase words with an underscore between each word; camelCase has no underscores but capitalizes the first letter of every new word in a compound string.

```
--for example

"hello_world" --snake_case

"helloWorld" --camelCase
```

Find a way for your code to find an underscore in the string and use it to determine where to capitalize. Refer to the string management functions from #3 if you're stuck.

#8 – RECAMÁN'S SEQUENCE

Recamán's sequence is a famous mathematical sequence that's made by subtracting the next index from the previous value. If the subtraction results in a value that is negative or already in the pattern, the index is added to the previous value instead. To illustrate how it works:

```
--Recaman's sequence
R = {0, 1, 3, 6, 2, 7, 13, 20, 12, 21, 11, 22, 10, 23, 9}
--[[ [0] = 0
     [1] = 1 (0 - 1 fails, therefore 0 + 1)
     [2] = 3 (1 - 2 fails, therefore 1 + 2)
     [3] = 6 (3 - 3 fails, therefore 3 + 3)
     [4] = 2 (6 - 2 succeeds)
     [5] = 7 (2 - 5 fails, therefore 2 + 5)
]]
```

For more on the sequence itself, try looking it up on YouTube.

Your challenge is to create an algorithm that will calculate these values without you supplying the numbers. Write code that will subtract the index from the previous value. If that results in a negative value or an existing value, it should add the index to the previous value. Use loops and conditionals to cycle through terms and use variables to represent the indexes. Display each new term and store it into an array.

#9 – NON-DECREASING ARRAYS

A non-decreasing array is any array where all elements are lesser than or equal to the element that follows them. In other words, they follow the rule array[k] <= array [k+1]. For example:

```
array1 = {2, 3, 6, 9} --non-decreasing array since each value is greater than the one before it
array2 =  {6, 5, 8, 9} --not a non-decreasing array since 6 is not lesser than 5
```

Write code that will test whether an array is non-decreasing. Use the rule above to test each element of an array with a for loop. Tip: Instead of testing it exactly as is, test whether [k] is greater than [k + 1], and any arrays that succeed this condition fail the non-decreasing test. If you want to add more to this challenge, try to figure out a way to test whether arrays that fail can become non-decreasing with change to a single element.

#10 – DRAW MULTIPLICATION

For this challenge, write code that will print a multiplication problem as you would if you wrote it out. To illustrate:

```
--go from this
 (5,4)


 --to this
     5
 x   4
 ======
    20
```

This uses a combination of string manipulation and arithmetic. If you want to make this even more challenging, code your function to calculate and display the equation like you would for long multiplication. For example:

```
--go from this
(452,21)

--to this
   452
x   21
=======
   452
+ 9040
=======
  9492
```

If you're unsure how to approach this, look up the steps to long multiplication and consider how you would tell a program to do them.

Help Spread the Gaming Passion!

Your problem-solving skills are improving. And as you develop your coding and gaming skills, you begin to see just how much potential you have. Whether your goal is to create a solid profile or some extra income, it's happening. And now it's time to let others see just what they are capable of.

You know how much of a difference a single click can make! I would be super grateful if you could add one more click for the day and share your opinion with others. One click and one minute can make a huge impact – but who am I telling? Happy gaming!

Scan the QR code for a quick review.

CONCLUSION

If you made it this far, well done! Really, you did a lot to get to this point, and it's something to be proud of. How does it feel to not only have new skills but also to have made two different, functional experiences? From one self-taught developer to another, this is only the beginning. You stand on the threshold of an incredible opportunity. We all start somewhere, and you've just started your journey.

Many people want to become a game developer or to make the next big game, but not many people actually take the steps to see it through. You did, and now you're ready for the next step. This isn't the end of your journey—not by far. There are still more things to learn, techniques to master, and experiences to explore. You have the tools to meet life as a Roblox developer head-on. Use what you've learned and grow beyond it. Experiment, be creative, and never stop developing your skills and interests.

If you enjoyed this book or found it at all helpful, please consider leaving a review. I'd love to hear your thoughts.

GLOSSARY

- **Anonymous function:** a function with no defined name; often used as parameters or linked to other functions and methods.
- **Arguments/Parameters:** variables through which information is passed from one area of code to another.
- **Array:** a table of data values listed in a specific order as indicated by a numerical index.
- **Compiled:** a process in which code is translated into machine language for execution.
- **Compiled language:** a programming language that requires code to be compiled before execution.
- **Condition:** a comparison of different values to return a value of true or false.
- **Data types:** each value or object is classed into a data type depending on what information it is or what it can be used for.

    - **Boolean:** a value that is either true or false.
    - **Function:** a code object that groups different code statements aimed at executing a goal.
    - **Nil:** the absence of any other value.
    - **Number:** any numerical value, both decimal and whole.
    - **String:** a collection of characters contained in quotation marks.
    - **Table:** a collection of related values, objects, functions,

and variables.

- **Thread:** references to threads of execution.
- **Userdata:** data that refers to individual users.

- **Debounce:** a boolean value used to stop events from repeatedly firing.
- **Dictionary:** a table that groups multiple values together, where each is identified by a unique key.
- **Element:** an entry in an array.
- **Elseif:** code that can be added onto an if-statement to provide an alternative condition.
- **Experience:** a game hosted on the Roblox platform.
- **Event:** something that occurs in response to a user interaction or when something happens in the game.
- **Event handler:** a function that is dedicated to managing an event.
- **Function:** a collection of code statements unified under a single name.
- **Humanoid:** a child object that is added to a player's character once they join an experience.
- **If-statement:** a statement in which a condition is tested to determine whether code should execute.
- **Instance:** the process by which an object is created from a preexisting class or module.
- **Interpreted language:** a programming language that's not compiled before execution but instead interpreted at run-time.
- **Ipairs:** a function that is used in for loops with arrays.

- **Key:** an identifying value used to distinguish members of a dictionary.
- **Loop:** a coding technique that lets code be repeated on the basis of a condition or controller.
- **Method:** a function that requires itself or parent object as parameter.
- **ModuleScript:** a script in which members are grouped inside a module object.
- **Obby:** a Roblox obstacle course.
- **Pairs:** a function that is used in for loops with dictionaries.
- **Parent-child:** a relationship that illustrates the connection between objects and structure in which they exist.
- **Part:** a visual object that can be added into an experience.
- **ReplicatedStorage:** a project service that contains objects meant to be involved in client-server communication.
- **Robux:** the virtual currency used in Roblox.
- **Script:** a container for code.
- **ServerScriptService:** a project service that contains objects that communicate exclusively on the server side of the client-server barrier.
- **ServerStorage:** a project service that stores objects used in accordance with server management.
- **Variable:** a container for unspecified values.
- **Variadic function:** a function that can take a varying number of arguments.

REFERENCES

AlvinBlox. (2018, April 9). *Roblox debounce tutorial.* [Video]. YouTube. https://www.youtube.com/watch?v=HoZkuvd6RPA.

Ben. (2021, September 13). *What's the difference between an array and a table?* https://devforum.roblox.com/t/whats-the-difference-between-an-array-and-a-table/1466701.

Bibard, F. (2021, August 23). *The easy guide to French numbers.* Talkinfrench.com. https://www.talkinfrench.com/french-numbers/.

Bindable events and functions. (n.d.). Create.roblox.com. https://create.roblox.com/docs/scripting/events/bindable-events-and-functions.

BindableFunction. (n.d.). Create.roblox.com. https://create.roblox.com/docs/reference/engine/classes/BindableFunction.

Boylls, T. (2023, January 24). *How to use Roblox Studio (with pictures).* WikiHow. https://www.wikihow.com/Use-Roblox-Studio.

Brumbaugh, Z. (2021). *Introducing Roblox development.* In Coding Roblox Games Made Easy. Packt. https://subscription.packtpub.com/book/game-development/9781800561991/2/ch02lvl1sec05/discovering-developer-types.

Buying upgrades. (n.d.). Create.roblox.com. https://create.roblox.com/docs/education/adventure-game-series/buying-upgrades.

CharlieJ. (2021, March 20). T*he beginners guide to all things game development.* DevForum. https://devforum.roblox.com/t/the-beginners-guide-to-all-things-game-development/1121665.

Cleanup and reset. (n.d.). Create.roblox.com. https://create.roblox.com/docs/education/battle-royale-series/cleanup-and-reset.

Coding the game loop. (n.d.). Create.roblox.com. https://create.roblox.com/docs/education/battle-royale-series/coding-the-game-loop#gamesettings-script.

Coding the leaderboard. (n.d.). Create.roblox.com. https://create.roblox.

com/docs/education/adventure-game-series/code-the-leader board.

Codotaku. (2018, November 10). *Variadic functions in Roblox Studio (Lua).* [Video]. https://youtu.be/KyX3HkEzZHI.

Collecting items. (n.d.). Create.roblox.com. https://create.roblox.com/docs/education/adventure-game-series/collect-items#troubleshooting-tips-1.

Color3. (n.d.). Create.roblox.com. https://create.roblox.com/docs/reference/engine/datatypes/Color3#fromRGB.

Create & Learn Team. (2022a, September 1). *How to make an obby in Roblox.* Kids' Coding Corner | Create & Learn. https://www.create-learn.us/blog/how-to-make-an-obby-in-roblox/.

Create & Learn Team. (2022b, September 26). *How to use conditional statements (if, then) in Roblox Studio.* Kids' Coding Corner | Create & Learn. https://www.create-learn.us/blog/conditional-statements-roblox-studio/.

Create on Roblox. (n.d.-a). Create.roblox.com. https://create.roblox.com/docs/tutorials/scripting/basic-scripting/intro-to-scripting.

Create on Roblox. (n.d.-b). Create.roblox.com. https://create.roblox.com/docs/education/adventure-game-series/landing.

Create the map. (n.d.). Create.roblox.com. https://create.roblox.com/docs/education/adventure-game-series/create-the-map.

Creating a battle royale. (n.d.). Create.roblox.com. https://create.roblox.com/docs/education/battle-royale-series/landing.

Creating a GUI. (n.d.). Create.roblox.com. https://create.roblox.com/docs/education/battle-royale-series/creating-a-gui.

Creating a Script. (n.d.). Create.roblox.com. https://create.roblox.com/docs/education/coding-1/creating-a-script.

Curry, D. (2023, February 28). *Roblox revenue and usage statistics* (2021). Business of Apps. https://www.businessofapps.com/data/roblox-statistics/.

Danmaigoro, A. S. (2021, September 3). *What are conditional statements in programming?* Educative: Interactive Courses for Software Developers. https://www.educative.io/answers/what-are-conditional-statements-in-programming.

DeepAI. (2020, June 25). *Pattern Matching.* DeepAI. https://deepai.org/machine-learning-glossary-and-terms/pattern-matching.

Developer economics | Roblox creator documentation. (n.d.). Create.roblox.com. https://create.roblox.com/docs/production/monetization/economics.

Dodge, D. (2022, May 12). *The ultimate guide to making your first game on roblox studio.* CodaKid. https://codakid.com/ultimate-guide-making-your-first-game-on-roblox-studio/.

Ending matches. (n.d.). Create.roblox.com. https://create.roblox.com/docs/education/battle-royale-series/ending-matches.

Events. (n.d.). Create.roblox.com. https://create.roblox.com/docs/scripting/events.

Finishing the project. (n.d.-a). Create.roblox.com. https://create.roblox.com/docs/education/adventure-game-series/finishing-the-project.

Finishing the project. (n.d.-b). Create.roblox.com. https://create.roblox.com/docs/education/battle-royale-series/finishing-the-project.

Functions. (n.d.). Create.roblox.com. https://create.roblox.com/docs/scripting/luau/functions.

Gorosae. (2022). *StarterTool.* https://create.roblox.com/marketplace/asset/10837098513/StarterTool.

Grubb, J. (2013, January 22). *Roblox in 2012: Users played for over 176 million hours.* VentureBeat. https://venturebeat.com/games/roblox-in-2012-users-played-for-over-176-million-hours/.

*Guiding your up-and-coming Roblox developer. (2023, February 17). Roblox Support. https://en.help.roblox.com/hc/en-us/arti*cles/4438648708756-Guiding-Your-Up-and-Coming-Roblox-Developer.

How to make an obby on Roblox. (2023, February 24). WikiHow. https://www.wikihow.com/Make-an-Obby-on-Roblox.

Ierusalimschy, R. (2003). *Programming in Lua (1st ed.).* Lua.org, Cop. https://www.lua.org/pil/contents.html#P1.

Ierusalimschy, R., De Figueiredo, L. H., & Celes, W. (2022). *Lua 5.4 Reference Manual.* Lua.org. https://www.lua.org/manual/5.4/contents.html#index.

Ierusalimschy, R. (n.d.). *Programming in Lua: 1.3.* Www.lua.org. https://www.lua.org/pil/1.3.html.

If/then practice with powerups. (n.d.). Create.roblox.com. https://create.roblox.com/docs/education/coding-3/powerups-with-if-statements.

If/then practice with traps. (n.d.). Create.roblox.com. https://create.roblox.com/docs/education/coding-3/traps-with-if-statements.

Instance. (n.d.). Create.roblox.com. https://create.roblox.com/docs/reference/engine/classes/Instance.

Intro to arrays. (n.d.). Create.roblox.com. https://create.roblox.com/docs/education/coding-5/intro-to-arrays.

Intro to dictionaries. (n.d.). Create.roblox.com. https://create.roblox.com/docs/education/coding-5/intro-to-dictionaries.

Intro to for loops. (n.d.). Create.roblox.com. https://create.roblox.com/docs/education/coding-4/intro-to-for-loops.

Intro to if statements. (n.d.). Create.roblox.com. https://create.roblox.com/docs/education/coding-3/intro-to-if-statements.

Intro to Module Scripts. (n.d.). Create.roblox.com. https://create.roblox.com/docs/education/coding-6/intro-to-module-scripts.

Isaac. (2016, July 7). *Roblox studio tour - episode 1: home section.* [Video]. Youtube. https://www.youtube.com/watch?v=VpTFBSNFynk.

Kenlon, S. (2022, November 30). *Get to know Lua for loops in 4 minutes.* Opensource.com. https://opensource.com/article/22/11/lua-for-loops.

Landsberg, N. (2022, September 14). *56 amazing Roblox statistics: Revenue, usage & growth stats.* Influencer Marketing Hub. https://influencermarketinghub.com/roblox-stats/.

Layn333, & MrNicNacWIKI. (2010, June 18). *Loops.* Roblox Lua Wiki. https://arebeexlua.fandom.com/wiki/Loops.

Litt, S. (n.d.). *Callback functions in Lua.* Www.troubleshooters.com. http://www.troubleshooters.com/codecorn/lua/luacallbacks.htm.

Loops and arrays. (n.d.). Create.roblox.com. https://create.roblox.com/docs/education/coding-5/loops-and-arrays.

Loops. (n.d.). Create.roblox.com. https://create.roblox.com/docs/education/coding-4/landing.

Loops practice - creating a timed bridge. (n.d.). Create.roblox.com. https://create.roblox.com/docs/education/coding-4/creating-a-timed-bridge.

Loops practice - glowing lights with for loops. (n.d.). Create.roblox.com. https://create.roblox.com/docs/education/coding-4/glow-lights-with-for-loops.

Lua array length | quick glance on Lua array length. (2021, May 19). Educba. https://www.educba.com/lua-array-length/.

Lua - arrays. (n.d.). Www.tutorialspoint.com. https://www.tutorialspoint.com/lua/lua_arrays.htm.

Lua - data types. (n.d.). Www.tutorialspoint.com. https://www.tutorialspoint.com/lua/lua_data_types.htm.

Lua - math library. (n.d.). Www.tutorialspoint.com. https://www.tutorialspoint.com/lua/lua_math_library.htm.

Lua - variables. (n.d.). Www.tutorialspoint.com. https://www.tutorialspoint.com/lua/lua_variables.htm.

Making changes to arrays. (n.d.). Create.roblox.com. https://create.roblox.com/docs/education/coding-5/making-changes-to-arrays.

Managing players. (n.d.). Create.roblox.com. https://create.roblox.com/docs/education/battle-royale-series/managing-players.

ModuleScripts. (n.d.). Create.roblox.com. https://create.roblox.com/docs/scripting/scripts/modulescripts.

Monetization | Roblox creator documentation. (n.d.). Create.roblox.com. https://create.roblox.com/docs/production/monetization.

MrNicNacWIKI, & Griffboy11. (2010, June 18). *Using an if statement.* Roblox Lua Wiki. https://arebeexlua.fandom.com/wiki/Using_an_If_Statement.

Multiple conditions with else/if. (n.d.). Create.roblox.com. https://create.roblox.com/docs/education/coding-3/multiple-conditions.

Nandanwar(Khadgi), J. (2022, September 30). *Roblox programming: A tool to learn coding.* ELearning Industry. https://elearningindustry.com/roblox-programming-a-tool-to-learn-coding.

Nested loops. (n.d.). Create.roblox.com. https://create.roblox.com/docs/education/coding-4/nested-loops.

Object properties. (n.d.). Create.roblox.com. https://create.roblox.com/docs/education/coding-1/object-properties.

Obstacle course. (2023, January 1). Roblox Wiki. https://roblox.fandom.

com/wiki/Obstacle_course.

Otaris, M. (2018, March 17). *Callback.* Roblox Wiki. https://roblox.fandom.com/wiki/Callback.

Parameters practice - buttons. (n.d.). Create.roblox.com. https://create.roblox.com/docs/education/coding-2/parameters-practice-buttons.

Parents and children. (n.d.). Create.roblox.com. https://create.roblox.com/docs/education/coding-1/parents-and-children.

Parts. (n.d.). Create.roblox.com. https://create.roblox.com/docs/building-and-visuals/studio-modeling/parts.

Paul. (2021, March 19). *Coding with kids. Coding with Kids.* https://www.codingwithkids.com/blog/2021/03/roblox-programming-parents-guide.html.

Repeating code with while loops. (n.d.). Create.roblox.com. https://create.roblox.com/docs/education/coding-4/repeating-code-with-while-loops.

Roblox_Educators. (2022). *Battle royale weapon.* https://create.roblox.com/marketplace/asset/10202913115/Battle-Royale-Weapon.

Roblox_Educators. (2022). *Graybox assets.* https://create.roblox.com/marketplace/asset/10202876758/Graybox-Assets.

Roblox Studio. (2023, February 17). *Roblox Support.* https://en.help.roblox.com/hc/en-us/articles/203313860-Roblox-Studio.

ropeccool. (2020). *Pink crystal.* https://create.roblox.com/marketplace/asset/5359904478/Pink-Crystal.

Rotate matrix elements. (2023, March 30). GeeksforGeeks. https://www.geeksforgeeks.org/rotate-matrix-elements/.

Selling items. (n.d.). Create.roblox.com. https://create.roblox.com/docs/education/adventure-game-series/selling-items.

ServerScriptService. (n.d.). Create.roblox.com. https://create.roblox.com/docs/reference/engine/classes/ServerScriptService.

Snap to grid. (n.d.). https://create.roblox.com/docs/education/build-it-play-it-create-and-destroy/snap-to-grid.

Sorting algorithms. (2023, March 21). GeeksforGeeks. https://www.geeksforgeeks.org/sorting-algorithms/?ref=lbp.

Starmaq. (2020a, March 16). *List of coding challenges.* DevForum.

https://devforum.roblox.com/t/list-of-coding-challenges/485248.

Starmaq. (2020a, March 28). *Coding challenge #1: Numbers to French.* Devforum.roblox.com. https://devforum.roblox.com/t/coding-challenge-1-numbers-to-french/500012.

Starmaq. (2020b, April 20). *Coding challenge #2: It's sorting time!* DevForum. https://devforum.roblox.com/t/coding-challenge-2-its-sorting-time/533472.

Starmaq. (2020b, May 17). *Coding challenge #4: Non-repeating character.* Devforum.roblox.com. https://devforum.roblox.com/t/coding-challenge-4-non-repeating-character/580162/3.

Starmaq. (2020c, May 18). *Coding challenge #5: Rotating 90-degrees.* Devforum.roblox.com. https://devforum.roblox.com/t/coding-challenge-5-rotating-90-degrees/581975.

Starmaq. (2020d, May 25). *Coding challenge #6: First duplicate.* Devforum.roblox.com. https://devforum.roblox.com/t/coding-challenge-6-first-duplicate/593935.

Starmaq. (2020e, May 30). *Coding challenge #7: Pairs divisible by 5.* Devforum.roblox.com. https://devforum.roblox.com/t/coding-challenge-7-pairs-divisible-by-5/601127.

Starmaq. (2020f, July 12). *Coding challenge #8: snake_case to camelCase.* Devforum.roblox.com. https://devforum.roblox.com/t/coding-challenge-8-snakecase-to-camelcase/668949.

Starmaq. (2020g, July 13). *Coding challenge #9: Recamán's sequence.* Devforum.roblox.com. https://devforum.roblox.com/t/coding-challenge-9-recam%C3%A1ns-sequence/670384/3.

Starmaq. (2020h, July 20). *Coding challenge #11: Non-decreasing arrays.* Devforum.roblox.com. https://devforum.roblox.com/t/coding-challenge-11-non-decreasing-arrays/680261.

Starmaq. (2020i, July 28). *Coding challenge #12: Draw the multiplication.* Devforum.roblox.com. https://devforum.roblox.com/t/coding-challenge-12-draw-the-multiplication/694622.

Stieg, C. (2022, November 16). *Why Lua is so popular — & what you can make with it.* Codecademy News. https://www.codecademy.com/resources/blog/what-is-lua-programming-language-used-for/.

String. (n.d.). Create.roblox.com. https://create.roblox.com/docs/refer

ence/engine/libraries/string#match.

Tables. (n.d.). Create.roblox.com. https://create.roblox.com/docs/scripting/luau/tables.

TechTarget Contributor. (2021, December 15). *What is loop?* WhatIs.com. https://www.techtarget.com/whatis/definition/loop.

Thundermaker300, & Otaris, M. (2021, July 18). *Dealing with debounce.* Roblox Wiki. https://roblox.fandom.com/wiki/Tutorial:Dealing_with_debounce.

Timers and events. (n.d.). Create.roblox.com. https://create.roblox.com/docs/education/battle-royale-series/timers-and-events.

Toolbox. (n.d.). Create.roblox.com. https://create.roblox.com/docs/studio/toolbox#asset-inspection.

Using events. (n.d.). Create.roblox.com. https://create.roblox.com/docs/scripting/events/using-events.

Variables. (n.d.). Create.roblox.com. https://create.roblox.com/docs/scripting/luau/variables.

Wickramasinghe, S. (2021, June 4). *The Lua programming language beginner's guide.* BMC Blogs. https://www.bmc.com/blogs/lua-programming-language/.

101 inspirational quotes about gaming & life. (2023, February 23). *Gracious Quotes.* https://graciousquotes.com/gaming/

Printed in Great Britain
by Amazon

29861055R00166